Ever heard a really tough-to-[...] some wise, biblically knowledgeable person would explain it? Me too. Lucky for both of us, I've found just the guy. In his new and long-awaited book, *Crazy Stories, Sane God*, my friend John Alan Turner educates and entertains as he sagely and sometimes hilariously explains some of the strangest stories in Scripture. If you read this book, you'll be in his debt. But I checked, and he doesn't mind.

—Eric Metaxas, *New York Times* best-selling author of
Bonhoeffer: Pastor, Martyr, Prophet, Spy and *7 Men: and the
Secret of their Greatness*

In the past several years, John Alan Turner and I have collaborated on a number of projects, and I have always been impressed with his writing skills, fresh insights, and practical acuity. His new book *Crazy Stories, Sane God* is a tour de force of these qualities applied to some of the most bizarre stories of the Bible. It combines innovative angles, fresh and unusual insights, and creative turns in the process of exploiting ironic twists and turning the craziness of sin into the sanity of salvation.

—Dr. Kenneth Boa, author *Conformed to His Image,
Faith Has It's Reasons,* and *An Unchanging
Faith in a Changing World*

You've probably heard about the time God parted the sea, but have you heard about the time He chucked ice cubes?

You've probably heard of the golden calf, but have you heard about the golden hemorrhoids?

You've heard that He can make the blind see and the deaf speak, but what about letting a donkey see the invisible and talk better sense than her master?

Get ready for some surprises. "My ways are not your ways," says the Lord.

The Bible is full of outrageous stories—even downright offensive stories. Are you going to whitewash over them and pretend God's Word is all ponies and flowers and sweetness? Or are you going to face God's Word for what it is? John Alan Turner knows his Bible well and he'll take you on a tour of some places you've probably not been. Fortunately, he also knows our Lord well and knows how to help us spot Him even in the dark. He'll show you that even the weirdest passages of Scripture contain clues to the beautiful, steadfast love of God. To read even a dozen pages of this book is to become convinced, with Turner, that "there is nothing—and I mean absolutely nothing—God cannnot redeem and use." I loved this book.

—Conrad Gempf, PhD,
Lecturer in New Testament Exegesis,
London School of Theology, author of
Jesus Asked and *How to Like Paul Again*

John Alan Turner has given the church a great gift in his newest release. Part theologian, part storyteller, Turner has the ability to keep the story simple without simplifying the mystery of God at work in the messes of our lives. I grew up listening to the stories of Israel, Jesus, and the early church.

Thanks to Turner, I now have another tool to use to ensure my children will be captivated by the story. Devour this book, let God inside your bones.

—Dr. Josh Graves, author of *The Feast*, *Heaven on Earth*, and *Tearing Down the Walls*

In *Crazy Stories, Sane God* John Alan Turner challenges us to stop analyzing and start worshipping the complete God of the complete Bible. These neglected stories remind us that God is both totally faithful and totally unpredictable. That's why His compassions are fresh every morning. The moment we figure God out and box Him in to our favorite theological system is the moment we remake Him in our own image and downgrade His glory to just another created being.

—Phil Tuttle, President, Walk Thru the Bible

One colorful country pundit observed, "There ain't no 'Biblical Characters' in the Bible! Only ordinary folks, who just happened to be standin' around when the Bible got wrote." John Alan Turner's refreshing book *Crazy Stories, Sane God*, confirms this notion. His raw and breezy style brings those Bible people to life on your own block—even in your own skin! At the same time, Turner also deftly unveils some transformative glimpses of God; glimpses that may grip your gaze—and hold it for a lifetime. The pages flew by.

—Lynn Anderson, President of Hope Network, author of *They Smell Like Sheep*

CRAZY
STORIES
SANE GOD

JOHN ALAN TURNER

CRAZY

STORIES

SANE GOD

LESSONS FROM THE MOST
UNEXPECTED PLACES IN THE BIBLE

B&H
PUBLISHING GROUP
NASHVILLE, TENNESSEE

978-1-4336-8128-8

Published by B&H Publishing Group
Nashville, Tennessee

Dewey Decimal Classification: 220
Subject Heading: BIBLE STORIES \ GOD \
CHRISTIAN LIFE

1 2 3 4 5 6 7 8 • 18 17 16 15 14

To David, Dane, and Hall—three guys I am honored to say have lived this crazy story with me.

Acknowledgments

ANY OF YOU who are connected with me on Facebook or Twitter know that I like to crowdsource things. That being the case, it's difficult for me to remember exactly who helped me come up with the list of stories in this book, the titles for those stories, the title of the book—even the cover of the book! So, if you were one of the many people who weighed in on anything having to do with this book, consider yourself thanked!

That means you, Daniel and Tim and Matt and Les and Nick and Dee Ann and Lisa and Brent and Jerry and Janna and Angie and Jeff and Julie and . . . well . . . you get the picture.

There are also people I should mention because I've stolen things from them—more things than I can remember. I'm talking about Stephen Mansfield and Andy Stanley and John Ortberg and Scot McKnight and Conrad Gempf and Philip Yancey. More than words or phrases, I've stolen from them a way of thinking. I won't be giving it back, but I wanted to confess here.

I am deeply indebted to some great thinkers—now departed—C. S. Lewis, Dallas Willard, and John Stott. I never met any of them, but I am looking forward to it in the life to come.

And then I am indebted to several mentors through the years—people who have helped me become who I am— people like Jefferson Walling, Christopher Green, Ken Boa, Steve Paden, and Rick Hazelip.

Of course, Eric Metaxas, Lynn Anderson, and Alex Field, great men of God who consistently treat me as if I am far more important than I really am.

I owe an incredible debt of gratitude to Sean Palmer and Angie Gray Fann. Without their help this book would never have gotten finished.

I have the best agent I know of: Andrew Wolgemuth. He concentrates on the business side so I can just write and not have to worry. That is an amazing gift. Oh, and thanks to Erik Wolgemuth for his work in helping realize my relationship with B&H.

Acknowledgments

Speaking of B&H, thanks to Dawn Woods and Dave Schroeder for their faith and patience. I have never been treated as well by a publisher, and I look forward to seeing how God uses this whole thing to bless people.

Special thanks to David Blackwell, Dane Booth, and Hal Runkel for the always appreciated sanity maintenance that is Guys Night Out.

Finally, I want to thank the folks at Shannon Oaks Church, Piedmont Church, the North Atlanta Church of Christ, The Bridge, and Stonecreek Church (especially my good friend and pastor Steven Gibbs) for letting me tell so many of these stories in public. In a world where it has become fashionable to bash churches, it is good to know there are churches who aren't afraid of "deep" and are still willing to wrestle with hard stuff.

Contents

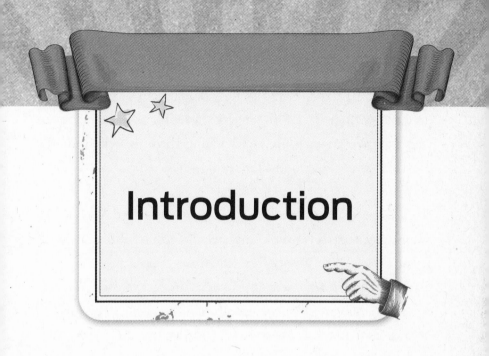

Introduction

I KNOW A lot of Bible stories. Noah's ark. Abraham and Isaac. Jonah and the whale. The birth of Jesus. The conversion of Saul. These stories are told anywhere, from popular literature to your local church. Every child hears these stories. They make movies about these stories. We've heard them so many times, we're sure we know what they mean.

But think about these stories. God killed everyone on earth except one family who survived in a boat and took two of every animal with them. God told a man to kill his only son. Jonah was swallowed by a giant fish and lived to tell about it. God became a fetus. A religious terrorist switched sides and became the greatest evangelist of all time.

Those stories are crazy, and one of the craziest things about them is that we tend to talk about them as if they're perfectly normal. Try telling one of those stories to someone who isn't part of our club, or try telling them to a child for the first time. You'll quickly realize these stories are not normal.

There are more. There are stories preachers and Sunday school teachers skip over completely. We don't talk much about these stories. VeggieTales could never pull off an animated, child-friendly version of these; in fact, we tend to change the subject quickly when our children bring them up because we don't know what to do with them or why they're in the Bible or what they could possibly mean.

Some of these stories would probably get an R-rating. Others blow our notions of family values to smithereens, like when Moses' wife circumcises her son and throws the foreskin at Moses. What's up with that? And then there's the time a prophet calls a couple of bears out of the woods to maul a gang of rowdy teenagers. Try using that one in your high-school ministry when things get a bit out of hand! Or how about the woman who dresses up like a prostitute and tricks her father-in-law into getting her pregnant. And their son ends up in the genealogy of Jesus!

What are we to make of these strange, sometimes cryptic, sometimes off-color stories? What are they doing in the Bible? And what about the stories where God seems to be doing things that contradict our understanding of what He's like . . . say, when He orders the Israelites to kill every man, woman, and child in Jericho? Or when God tells one of His prophets to marry a prostitute? Or when two of the earliest Christians get struck down for telling a lie?

These stories are never presented on a flannel board in Vacation Bible School. In fact, they hardly ever get told at all. But God put them in the Bible for a reason, and it's time we do what it takes to try to understand them. We actually do God, our families, and ourselves a disservice when we gloss over these stories or pretend they're not in there.

What you're about to read is not safe for the whole family. There are grown-up stories in here. This will be a wild and unpredictable ride through some of the weirdest and least familiar stories in the Bible. But through it all, I hope to show you how even these odd episodes reveal important things about the character and nature of God and, consequently, what they mean for us today.

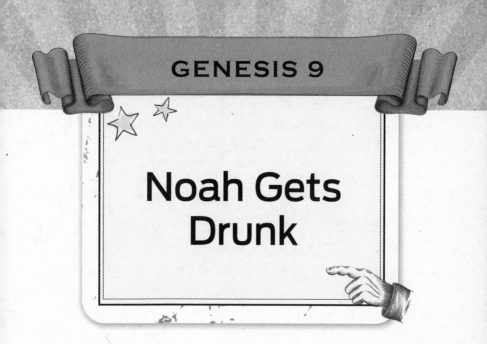

Noah Gets Drunk

A TIME CAME when God was sad that He'd made these humans who kept running around hurting themselves and others so He decided to start over. He found the best guy of his generation, a man named Noah. Then He gave Noah specific instructions about how to build a really big boat. Once Noah's construction began, obviously, the people around him were curious; they wanted to know what he was doing and, more important, why. This gave Noah the chance to explain to them: "God is displeased with the way we're doing things. He's asked me to build this boat because He's going to flood everything. If you like, you could join me in the boat, or we could ask God to hold off on the rain. Who knows? Maybe if we get enough folks to pray, God will change His mind." But no one listened. Noah preached

5

and preached, then built and built. And you know it had to be lonely. At least he had his family—his wife, his three sons, and their wives—all working together to preserve the human race. There aren't many higher callings than this.

One day Noah awoke to find a line of animals filing into the ark. He didn't go get them; the animals came to him. The animals had better sense than the people around Noah.

Then one day God said, "All aboard," so Noah and his family got in the boat. God closed the door behind them, and it started to rain. For forty days and forty nights. The rivers overran their banks; the tides surged; the creeks flooded. Water was everywhere, covering everything. And people died. They didn't have to, but they chose to ignore all the warnings.

Noah and his family were safe and sound with all of those animals in a big floating zoo. Eventually it stopped raining and the waters subsided. The sun came out and dried up the land. The animals were released. Noah and his family found their land legs again. While more than eight humans and a slew of animals were officially on that boat, there was a stowaway: sin. Buried deep within each of the human hearts sin was also preserved on that boat. And that sin would soon manifest itself in a very perverted sort of way.

Now, Noah was made of dust, just as Adam had been. The same dust that God had cursed after the first couple fell into sin. And like his ancestor, Noah was also a farmer. So, after the whole flood was over, one of the first things Noah did was plant a vineyard, grow some grapes, and make some wine. That first harvest must have been sweet. And the first taste of wine—the rich, loamy aroma—must have gone down easily. A little too easily, perhaps.

Noah gets drunk, gets naked, and passes out. One of Noah's sons, Ham, discovers him, and what happens next is odd. Instead of helping his father, Ham tells his brothers about it. The other two brothers, Shem and Japheth, have enough sense, common decency, and respect to go in there and cover their father up. When Noah comes out of his drunken stupor and realizes what has happened, he curses Ham's unborn grandson whose name happened to be . . . Canaan.

And such a curse it is! Canaan and, presumably, all of his descendants are going to be the lowest of slaves to his brothers and, presumably, all of their descendants. The sad irony is that Noah had been the recipient of God's undeserved mercy and grace. Those who receive such gifts from God ought to be great dispensers of the same. Noah proves that this isn't always the case.

Go Figure

I have a friend named Brent. He pastors in a denomination that leans a little left on the theological spectrum. Like all denominations his has baggage. For more than half a century, this denomination has devoted itself to the pursuit of social justice and advocacy of the poor; however, it has often done so at the expense of personal piety. So, while they may be quick to help people in need, they are also fairly loose with their morals. He tells me frequently that my sermons would not work there—that I hammer grace too much. It would give them the wrong idea. They've heard too much grace. They need to be called to account for their sin. They need a proper standard of holiness to instill in them an appropriate fear of the Lord. They need to hear hard truths about sin. And I sometimes wonder if Brent could preach at many of the places where I do because his messages might come across as legalistic.

It's ironic. Sometimes we wish we could swap baggage. I'd love to be the most conservative guy in the room for a bit, and I'm sure he gets tired of sounding like a cranky guy yelling at the kids for riding their bikes across the lawn. The grass is always greener—even at church. And speaking of greener grass and baggage . . . I assume you know what those expressions mean, and I assume you know they aren't meant to be taken literally. But, if someone were to pick up this book, say, four hundred years from now (or, worse, four thousand years from now), they might spend a lot of time trying to figure out how an entire denomination can lean to the left and carry baggage, or why their lawns are in such better shape than their ecclesiastical neighbors. Figures of speech are curious; they can help explain things in the short term but can end up obscuring things in the long term.

When the Bible says that Ham "saw his father naked" (Gen. 9:22), it doesn't seem like such a big deal; Noah seems to overreact. Cursing an entire branch of your family tree just because someone saw you naked? That's a bit much, isn't it? Stay with me, though.

According to the book of Leviticus (which we should remember was written by the same guy who wrote the book of Genesis, about the same time, using the same language and initially read by the same audience), this is kind of a euphemism for incest between a son and his mother. I did not make that up. It's in Leviticus 18:6–8 and Leviticus 20:11.

The Bible is not "safe for the whole family" and any accurate rendering of the stories in Genesis alone would be labeled "For Mature Audiences Only." Which brings me back to my friend Brent. He is envious that I "get to" preach grace as much as I do, and it is true that I preach grace a lot—more than some people like. Perhaps I did not hear enough of grace when I was growing up; I know too well both the lure and the sting of legalism. I also know too many people who live with an unhealthy sense of shame for the things they've done. I know personally how it can mess with your head and your heart, turning you into a destructively secret and insecure person. In today's church, as long as the consequences of being caught are the same as the consequences of confessing one's sin, secrecy will rule the day. We hide as if our lives depend on it, when the truth is, the opposite is true. In coming into the light with our sin, confident that God loves and God forgives, we find the life that is truly life.

And yet I would be remiss if I whitewashed over this story because it shows that sin, while it never gets to have the last word, does matter. Every so often we are forced to watch some Christian leader tragically fall before our very eyes; when that happens, I can't help but be unspeakably grateful that there weren't millions of people watching me at my darkest hour. I've fallen off my high horse more times than I can count, and for some strange reason I keep climbing back on it. I know what it's like to be caught in a lie and what it's like to be embarrassed or humiliated by the depths of my own depravity. I know what it's like to stare up from the bottom of a pit I dug with my own hands and wonder if I could ever get out, longing for the ability to fly backwards around the world, reverse time, and undo what I did. I just don't know what it's like to do that while the whole world is watching.

Stories like this present us with something profoundly simple, something most of us tend to overlook, something few of us want to admit but are forced to if we are to learn anything: sin is bad. Sin is worse than we think it is. Sin is the most awful and terrible of all things. Sin corrupts everything it touches, particularly relationships and character. While it corrupts the character of the one who sins, it also threatens to corrupt the character of the one who is sinned against. It's terribly contagious. Sin keeps us from experiencing the life for which we were created, the life we always wanted but never thought possible, life as it is supposed to be. Sin prevents us from entering into the joy of God, the peace of God, the rest and fulfillment He has purchased for us at immeasurable cost. Sin disrupts, destroys, and corrodes everything it touches. It is pervasive and persistent. It touches everything about us: our hearts, minds, bodies, feelings, thoughts, and actions. It has touched everything about our world: governments, businesses, families, and churches. There is not one part of me or of this world that is untainted by the disruptive effects of sin. Sin is far worse than words can describe.

And sin is what prompted God to destroy everyone but Noah and his family. Sin caused the flood and its collateral damage. Sin kills. It's far easier to analyze Ham's sin than it is to stare my own sin in the face and admit there's little wrong with him that isn't also wrong with me. Sin is not a problem; sin is *the* problem. And it's deeply imbedded in me.

Thankfully, this book is not about sin. This book is not about me, or Ham, or Noah, or the latest televangelist who got caught red-handed. No, this book is about God. So, what do we learn about God from this ugly story of twisted desire?

God does not take away sin, but He doesn't take away His blessing, either. And just as evil rolls across the ages, good does as well. The goodness of God has its own momentum, so the corrupting power of sin never completely succeeds. God's grace is truly greater than all our sin because, as stubborn as human sin may be, God is more stubborn and more persistent by far. He wants things the way they're supposed to be, and He will pay whatever price He must to get just that. God is willing to suffer to get what He wants; evil is not.

So even though sin is the problem, God is the solution. God's grace is not a way of resolving the problem provided we combine it with other things. God's grace is the once-and-for-all, paid-in-full, settled-for-good resolution. God's grace is not a solution: God's grace is *the* solution. And it's available in abundance to each and every one of us.

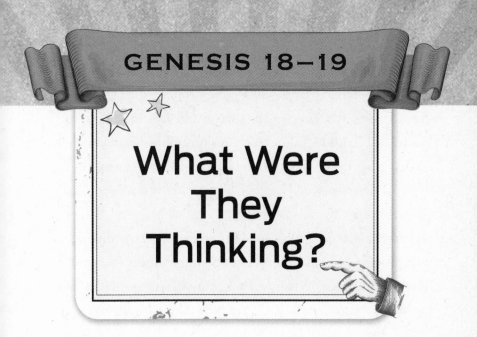

What Were They Thinking?

LOT WAS ABRAHAM'S nephew. That's where we have to begin. He's only famous because he's related to someone famous. Today he would be referred to as a male "celebutante" or hanger-on. And we don't really know why he chose to accompany his uncle on his strange journey of faith. Perhaps it was because he was convinced Uncle Abram actually heard something; or maybe Lot just saw this as a chance to start over somewhere new and get on with his own life. Whatever his reasons, when he is given the chance to choose which part of this promised land he wanted for his own, he chose an area known as Sodom. Yes, the namesake for the word *sodomy*.

13

Now this entire enterprise had been based on a promise Abraham received from God—the promise that he would have a son, that his descendants would live in a fantastic place, and that his children's children's children would eventually grow into a vast nation that would make the entire world a better place. The problem is, that promise took an awfully long time to materialize.

In the meantime Lot and Abraham are doing all right. Lot raises his family among the Sodomites and gets himself elected as a judge. When he finds himself in the middle of a war between two tribal groups, Uncle Abraham must rescue him.

For the most part, however, life is pretty good. His daughters grow up and find two nice Sodomite boys. They get engaged. Lot and Mrs. Lot are busy preparing for the wedding. And then it all unhinges.

God decides to destroy the city; but first, like a wise Judge, He sends a warning. He actually sends two angels (who look like regular men) to warn Lot. When the two men get to Lot's house, he invites them in. They say they don't want to be any bother; they're fine sleeping out on the street. Lot assures them they don't want to do that, begging them to come inside. They relent, but by now they've attracted the attention of all the other men in the city. Now the story gets a little unseemly.

The men in the city want Lot to send the two men/ angels outside for a little chat. Only it's not a chat they want. They want to engage in the kind of activity that is now known as sodomy. Lot rhetorically suggests they just take his virgin daughters and gang-rape them instead. The men are angry at this point and tell Lot that if he doesn't release the men to them, they're coming in after them . . . and Lot, too.

The angels strike the men of the city blind and command Lot to take his family and get out. Specifically, they were to leave the city and not look back until they were decidedly somewhere safe. Lot tries to talk his future sons-in-law into joining them, but it's no use. Everyone else in the city is corrupt beyond reform, so early the next morning, Lot, Mrs. Lot, and their two daughters leave. Along the way Mrs. Lot decides, "This is crazy! I'm going back." And she pays the ultimate price and turns into a pillar of salt. The city is wiped out. Lot and his daughters end up in a cave, probably wondering if they're the only people left on earth. And what happens next continues the unseemly theme of Lot's story.

The two daughters, perhaps assuming they are left alone with their father to repopulate the earth, get him drunk and have sex with him. And, in what can only be considered an ironic twist, they both end up pregnant while Abraham and Sarah continue to struggle with infertility issues. Now I don't know about you, but after this story I feel like I need go wash my mind out with soap.

Who Are You? Why Are You Here?

This wouldn't get past the television censors—it's beyond daytime drama. In stories like these we are most susceptible to falling into the trap of thinking these stories are about the people of God. They're not. These stories are about the God of the people, so let's keep that in the forefront and try to figure out what in the world we learn about God's character and nature from this story. A few things, actually.

First, when God told Abraham that He was going to destroy the city of Sodom, Abraham was concerned about his nephew and asked, "God, why would you destroy that city while there are good people in it?" God found this question entirely reasonable and told Abraham that if there were fifty righteous people in the city, He'd spare it. As they continued their discussion, God eventually agreed that if Abraham could even find ten righteous people in the city of Sodom, He would not destroy it. Of course, God already knew there weren't ten righteous people there, but He did engage Abraham in this conversation to show him that He is not unreasonable. God also wanted Abraham to know that He is not in a hurry to destroy cities and people because even just a few righteous people can make a difference in a city. This would be important for the descendants of Abraham to know as they begin the process of claiming their promised land. They were surrounded by terribly wicked people, but they were supposed to act like leaven in their society. They would need this lesson later when the Babylonians captured them, too. Just a few good people can make a difference in a nation of pagan people.

The early Christians would need to hear this, too. Imagine those folks coming together in Rome or Corinth to celebrate Jesus. They were under orders to go out into the wide world and share this message, but what hope was there of making an impact? Their cities were morally corrupt. This story showed them that they may be the reason God stayed His hand of judgment.

And finally, we need to hear this today. Sure, some of us live in places where everyone goes to one of the churches that appear on every single corner of town. But some of us live in places where Christians are few and far between, places where it can feel oppressive and dark. You need to know that you may be one of the ten righteous people in town. God has you there so you can make a difference. He believes it's possible. We also learn that there comes a time when God is done giving second chances. Once things have reached a "point of no return"—once a person or a society has crossed the line from which there is no turning back,

God will execute judgment; and, while that judgment may not be hasty, it will be swift.

Oh, and just a final mention about Lot and his daughters committing incest. While the girls succeed in getting pregnant by their father, which is horrible, incest was looked down upon by even the most pagan societies of the time. The Bible never condones actions like this, but nor does the Bible condemn these girls either. They were obviously traumatized and probably thought they were the last people on earth. Not that it makes it right, but it does provide possible insight into why they would initiate such actions. Their children are named Moab and Ammon, respectively; their descendants, obviously, become the Moabites and the Ammonites. One of the Moabites will be Ruth, and she is part of the genealogy of Christ. One of the Ammonites will be Naamah, and she marries a king named Solomon. They have a son named Rehoboam, who is also in the same genealogy. So the lineage of Jesus contains Moabites and Ammonites—people who were born out of an incestuous orgy between two sisters and their father. My point here is this: There is nothing, and I mean absolutely nothing, God can't redeem and use for His purposes—not even in cases of rape or incest. The promise of God is that everything gets wrapped up in His purposes, and—one day, in the distant future—we may well see good come out of something that seems horrible.

GENESIS 22

Is It Soup Yet?

"ABRAHAM?" CALLED THE Voice.

"Here I am," came the reply.

Of course, YHWH doesn't need directions. He knows where Abraham is, and the old man knows that. He's really saying, "At your service."

This Voice was maddening. It made amazing promises, but then it made impossible requests: leave everything you know; give up your status in the community; become a laughingstock; change your name; have yourself circumcised; go make a baby with your wife, who is nearly ninety. Oh, and one more thing—give up everything again, for the sake of the promise. What on earth could It want now?

"Give up the promise."

"What?"

"Take your son, your only son, Isaac, whom you love . . ."

"Yes, yes, yes. I know who you're talking about."

"And kill him."

The idea that the old couple would have a baby was laughable in the first place. Now the laughter is about to die.

Early the next morning Abraham gathers his things, chops some wood, and starts his journey. For three days the party walks together. Mostly in silence.

They reach a point, and he looks at his traveling companions. "Stay here. The boy and I are going over there to worship. We'll be right back."

Is he lying? It wouldn't be the first time. Does he wonder if he actually has what it takes to go through with it? Is he convinced that somehow there's got to be some alternate plan in the works? We don't know. He just keeps walking— tenaciously putting one foot in front of the other.

The boy has no idea that the wood he is carrying is the wood on which he will be killed. But Abraham, like a good father, carries the dangerous objects himself: the knife and the fire. Still, Isaac is old enough to do math. He knows something's not right, so he speaks up. "Dad?"

"Yes, my son." Literally, he says the same thing to Isaac that he had said to YHWH: "Here I am. I'm at your service. I'm completely available for you."

"Where is the animal we're going to sacrifice?"

"YHWH will provide," was the cryptic response he received.

It's not really an answer, but it will have to suffice. It's all Abraham can think of. And the two of them go on together—one carrying a physical burden, the other carrying an emotional one.

Bit by bit Abraham goes through the motions. He does things, perhaps mechanically, without thinking too much about the horror he is about to commit. He stacks the wood, fashions it into an altar. Then he binds the boy, placing his body there. He holds the knife and raises his hand.

And it must have felt like an eternity. It is supposed to feel like that.

Abraham never believed or obeyed perfectly; there was always a little skepticism at work. Regardless of his doubts or morality, however, he never runs or hides or goes to a different god; instead, he keeps taking step after excruciating step because somehow he believes this strange YHWH, who seems so terrible right now, will be the same YHWH who spoke so many wonderful things to him before. That somewhere in this story of blood and death will appear the YHWH who makes impossible promises and keeps them and names them "laughter."

"Abraham! Abraham!" comes another voice, calling his name twice with urgency. And for the third time, Abraham replies, "Here I am." As if to say, "Don't you know by now? I'm here. I'll do whatever you want."

"Now I know that you fear God and will do whatever He asks. Now I know that YHWH Himself is enough for you, that you will hold nothing back. Now I know that you're completely surrendered."

His boy is spared while a ram is caught in a thicket. Both father and son know something about this YHWH now that they didn't know before . . . and it shakes them to their core while it also changes the course of human history.

Soup or Nuts?

This is a crazy story in part because so many of us grew up hearing it and act as if it's a completely normal thing for God to ask. But this is not normal; it's bizarre. Having a baby wasn't even Abraham's idea in the first place; it was God's. And now He plays what appears to be a very cruel practical joke on an old man. Something's not right, either with the story itself or, more likely, with the way we've always read the story. And something's for sure not right with how casually we talk about it in Christian circles.

Maybe the whole key comes in the first sentence: "Sometime later, God tested Abraham." From the outset we're privy to some information Abraham did not have.

This is a test. This is only a test. The boy is never in any real danger. We know this; Abraham, of course, does not.

The concept of testing is important in the Bible. It only occurs with someone who is an insider—and passing the test isn't what makes you an insider; having to deal with the test is proof you are already there.

A word about this testing: sometimes it seems as if a teacher or professor is trying to catch his or her students napping by means of a pop quiz. "Aha! I caught you slacking off! Now you better shape up before the final exam gets here, or you'll really be in trouble." That's not how God tests His people. God's tests are categorically different.

I liken God's tests to how I approach cooking. There is something therapeutic about staring into a pot of red sauce simmering on the stove. Or a really thick soup with all sorts of tasty bits floating around. Add a little sausage, perhaps? And some wild rice? Maybe some parsley and black pepper.

Whatever is added, a really good soup will have the balance of flavors that hit you all at once. It can become impossible to discern what exactly is in there because it's all kind of married up and blended together. While you're making the soup, it's important to taste it periodically. Is it soup yet? Nope. It needs something . . . maybe more salt . . . more oregano . . . or maybe it just needs more time. And then comes that magic moment when it ceases to be random ingredients swimming in a pot and becomes a flavorful soup!

This is more like what God's tests are. Our faith is not downloaded into our brains in a finalized or completed version. Faith requires time. The kind of faith God wants has to simmer and steep for a while before it's soup.

It's fair to say that God is testing Abraham to see if his faith is "done" yet. There were other tests before this one, like when Abraham tells his wife to pretend she's his sister when they visit Egypt because he's afraid they'll kill him. Really he's afraid God won't protect him. Abraham's faith wasn't "soup" yet. Or the time his wife suggests he make a baby with her maid, Hagar. They're both afraid God's not really going to keep His promise to the two of them. Maybe He needs them to do some creative problem solving. Still not soup yet. Then the final exam: "Take your son, your only son, Isaac, whom you love, and kill him."

Why so many words? He could have just said, "Kill Isaac." And how ironic is it that Isaac's name means laughter? In the middle of this heavy and dark and sad story, there's laughter. From a human perspective there's always an element of absurdity to God's doings.

We're not told anything about how Abraham feels. We're told about the prompt and meticulous obedience. But surely there must have been some gut-wrenching thoughts and emotions churning inside of him. As far as we know, this is the last time God speaks to Abraham. The patriarch dies a couple of chapters later, but, other than that, we don't hear too much more about him.

Leading up to that moment, part of me wants to scream at my Bible (the way one might scream at a television or movie character): "It's going to be all right! This is just a test! He's not that kind of God!"

But Abraham wouldn't be able to hear me, and it would sort of ruin the adventure if he could. I can skip to the end of this story when my anxiety gets the better of me. Abraham couldn't do that. Abraham could only live life one verse at a time. And in a sense that's how we're called to live as well. I wish I could skip ahead and know how everything's going to turn out for me. I wish I could know that my kids will end up happily married with children of their own, fulfilling their vocation, and taking hold of God's best for them. That would certainly help us get through the teenage years. But I can't do that. None of us can.

What we discover is that faith is not doubt-free certainty or a rock-solid morality. More often than not faith is simply the staunch refusal to quit when it gets hard. Faith sometimes means walking patiently when everything inside of you screams, "Run!" And faith sometimes means you just keep walking when all you want to do is quit.

It took Abraham three days to find that ram. Those must have been the three longest days of Abraham's life. The

Bible is full of three-day stories, and one in particular happens almost two thousand years after Abraham and Isaac's ordeal. Another Son is forced to carry the wood on which He will be killed. Only He knows it. And this time there is no voice to stop the hand of the Father. The Son actually dies. Yet three days later . . . well, you know how that crazy story ends. And how its ending was actually the beginning for the rest of us.

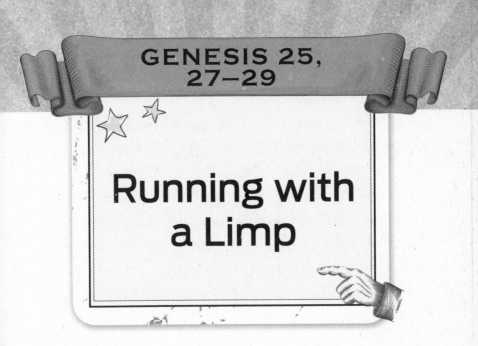

Running with a Limp

JACOB WAS A troublemaker before he was even born, wrestling with his twin brother Esau for the right to leave the womb first. Growing up, it was obvious that they were as different as night and day: Esau was an outdoorsman, a real man's man; Jacob, meanwhile, was the indoorsy type. Esau liked to hunt; Jacob liked to cook. Even their physical appearances were different: Esau was hairy; Jacob was not. Perhaps the most important difference for us to note is that Esau was impulsive and rash while Jacob was calculating and devious. And their father Isaac loved Esau, his firstborn.

One day Esau went out to hunt. He returned exhausted and famished to find his brother fussing over a pot of lentils. What a coincidence! The smell drove Esau mad with desire, and in his reckless state he promised Jacob his birthright in exchange for a bowl of soup.

Fast-forward just a bit. Now Jacob never could find the approval from his father his brother enjoyed, and his father was nearing the end of his life. Isaac was blind and on his deathbed. Concocting a plan with his mother, Jacob pretended to be Esau. His act fooled Isaac, and for a few moments Jacob knew what it was like to hear his father say how proud he was of him and how blessed he would be. But affirming words brought on by deception never linger for long.

Esau responded like a wounded animal, and their mother sent Jacob to her uncle's place, where he could lay low until the heat was off. Oh, but more trouble awaited him there!

As soon as Jacob arrived, he saw her. Rachel was beautiful. Jacob burst into tears at the sight of her—not the most macho thing to do—but he vowed then and there that he would do whatever it took to marry her. As it turned out, Rachel was Laban's daughter, and Laban's price for one of his daughters was seven years of work. Cue camera close-up of Laban's smirky smile while he stroked his beard greedily.

Jacob's love for Laban's daughter is so intense that the seven years seem to fly by. With the wedding ceremony over, Jacob is overjoyed until his wedding night. His wife enters the tent, wrapped in a veil, silent in the darkness. Turns out Jacob did not marry Rachel; he married her older sister, Leah, whose eyes were weak and whose face was not quite beautiful.

This is not right! Jacob was cheated out of what was rightfully his. He'd worked hard and honored his role in the agreement, and now he had been deceived . . . um, just like Esau . . . er uh, just like Isaac.

Now Laban's response is interesting. It basically boils down to something along these lines: "Maybe it's different where you come from, but around here we don't usually allow the grabby second-born child to jump in line ahead of the firstborn." So another agreement was reached; Jacob worked another seven years for the right to marry the daughter he wanted from the beginning. Fourteen years and two wives later, he leaves Laban's place having learned a difficult lesson about being on the receiving end of deception.

Jacob is ready to face his own music and either be reconciled to his brother or at least to die trying. Fourteen years in God's school of hard knocks has formed his character. He must pass one last final exam, however; as strange as this sounds, God wants to wrestle with Jacob.

All night long Jacob wrestles with . . . a man? An angel? I think it was God Himself. Jacob wrestles with God and gets a new name out of the bargain: Israel—the man who wrestled with God and lived to tell about it.

Too Familiar

I hate Jacob, and I hate his story.

I'm not supposed to say that, am I? It's true, though. Jacob was a schemer, a swindler, a manipulator, and a cheat. Frankly, it's surprising to me that people still name their sons after him. But the real reason I hate him is because of all the characters in the entire Bible, I identify with Jacob more than anyone else.

I digress . . . when I was a teenager, a friend of my father's was visiting. We all went out to a local high school track to run. This was southern California in the 1980s—everyone was a runner. My father's friend was accustomed to being the most in-shape guy around, but after about an hour of running with me, he looked at my father and said, "That boy is nothing but run." A pretty apt metaphor for my life for many years. I ran. A lot. From everyone and everything, from love, from consequences. Just like Jacob.

I wish I could say I resembled someone better than Jacob. David, maybe. Peter. Heck, I'd settle for the rich, young ruler or the kid who runs out of the garden of Gethsemane naked. But if I'm really honest, I am Jacob. I lie all the time—usually to get myself out of trouble or to make myself look better. Sometimes, though, I lie for no apparent reason. And I cheat. I manipulate. I hold grudges. I love the idea of people more than I actually love people (Jacob doesn't fall in love with Rachel at first sight; he falls in love with the idea of Rachel. Like Shakespeare's Romeo, he's in love with being in love.) And I run. Well, I used to run; now I limp. I am guilty of the same things as Jacob. I've learned not to lead with this information; it's not conducive to the hiring process, especially if your career is being a professional Christian. Churches don't hire a lot of Jacobs—at least, not on purpose.

Jacobs like me learn to hide our Jacobness. We wear masks and pretend. And we will outhustle anyone; we've learned to spot all the Labans and give them a wide berth until we can figure out how to get what we want from them and then get out of town. One thing we Jacobs know how to do, though: we know how to wrestle, especially with God.

Wrestling is different from fighting. A good wrestler can take down a man twice his size and pin him into submission because there is more at work than just brute strength or conditioning. Those things can be assets for a fighter, but a wrestler can survive on finesse and wits. Wrestlers have balance, quickness, and agility; and there are holds involved. If you can learn how to exploit your opponent's pressure points, you can take advantage of him. A wrestler is a thinker; he calculates things out. If fighting was checkers, then wrestling would be chess. Esau was a fighter; Jacob was a wrestler.

And, for reasons only He knows, it seems like God prefers wrestlers to fighters. Most of the time, when God comes across a fighter, He just puts the fighter down immediately. God doesn't like to fight so He ends it quickly. But God loves to wrestle, and He'll let you wrestle with Him for hours, days, weeks, years, decades. I have theories as to why this is, but they are only theories. What I know from both personal experience and from years of observation is this: ask God to fight, and you'll end up flat on your back before the last syllable exits your mouth; ask God to wrestle, and you better pack a lunch—you're going to be there all day.

One other thing I can tell you: we Jacobs don't wrestle with God because we lack faith. On the contrary, we wrestle with God precisely because we have faith. You don't wrestle with someone you don't believe exists, and you don't wrestle with God unless He disappoints you—which means you've got some expectations. If that's not faith, then what is?

My final thought about this story (and after this, I pray it mercifully leaves me alone for a while so I can move on and continue writing the rest of this book) is this: we Jacobs know we stole the birthright and the blessing, and things we gain through deception must be maintained by deception. Never mind the fact that God chose to bless Jacob before he was born. Never mind the fact that God could squash us if He chose to do so. We believe we got what we got through hustle, determination, and savvy, generally staying one step ahead of everyone else. So we live that way forever—trying to outmaneuver everyone. We survive by our wits and by being clever. We drive ourselves and everyone around us crazy because we feel the constant need to work for what we've been given. Secretly we know we don't deserve the blessings of heaven, and we think the only way we'll get in is either through some sort of clerical error or perhaps by tricking God—maybe find a loophole somewhere—taking Him in a game of three-card monte.

Somewhere in the dark recesses of our minds, we realize how futile and foolish this sounds and is. But we can't help ourselves. We are tricksters by nature. The only thing that will ever snap us out of it is when God, tired of wrestling with us, wounds us without killing us. Young Jacobs are "nothing but run," and old Jacobs all walk with a limp.

A Scandal for Christmas

JUDAH HAD THREE sons—nothing unusual about that. His oldest one married a woman named Tamar. The Bible doesn't tell us much about this oldest son except this: he was a bad apple. So bad, in fact, that God killed him. The second son was named Onan. He was expected to marry Tamar and get her pregnant, as was the custom back then. But Onan only wanted to have sex with her; if you're not already familiar with this story, read Genesis 38:9, and you'll know how he managed to do so without impregnating her. Hard to believe this is actually in the Bible, isn't it?

God didn't like the fact that Onan treated Tamar like an object. What Onan did was selfish and mean, so God killed him, too. To put it mildly, Tamar wasn't having very good luck with the guys. Now Judah had one more son, but he was way too young; they agreed that when the boy got old enough, he'd marry Tamar and do for her what neither of his older brothers accomplished. Until then she would live with her parents and wait. By now she must have felt like she was cursed, or damaged goods, or something because she actually agreed to go along with this.

Years went by. Tamar waited. The boy, Shelah, grew up. Judah's wife died, and he grieved the loss of two sons and a wife. Eventually his life and work resumed. Then, like a lot of men throughout history, Judah sought solace in the arms of a "professional" woman.

Although the woman's face was covered, it didn't matter. He propositions her.

"How much you got?" she asks.

He says, "What can I get in exchange for a goat?" Obviously, not the most romantic conversation, but they both know they're not there for romance—this was a business transaction. They go to some quiet place and do a goat's worth of whatever it is they do. And when they're done, she asks, "Where's my goat?"

"I don't have it with me, but I'll send it to you tomorrow."

"Yeah, right," she says and asks for his ring, cord, and staff for collateral. And Judah complies.

When he returns home, he sends the young goat. It's likely that this is not so much about honoring his end of the deal as much as he just wants his personal effects back. Especially since he tasks a friend to deliver the goat.

Trouble is his friend never finds the "cult prostitute" (Gen. 38:21). He asks around, and no one knows who she is because there wasn't a prostitute in the area. Eventually he returns to Judah with the goat and says, "I couldn't find her. What do you want to do?" Judah decides to leave it alone— if he makes a big deal out of her having his stuff, people will figure out how she got it.

A few months later someone mentions to Judah that Tamar is pregnant and adds a juicy tidbit that she's been acting like a prostitute. Judah is none too pleased; after all, she was supposed to save herself for young Shelah, and eventually he would have gotten around to fulfilling that long-ago promise, too. He orders her to be burned at the stake, which seems like a crazy, stereotypical overreaction for a guy who had visited a prostitute himself.

As they are taking her into custody, she sends a message and some items to Judah. The message is that her baby's father is the guy who gave her—wait for it—a ring, a cord, and a staff. Obviously, Judah now knew who was responsible. He drops the charges and acknowledges his failure to honor his initial agreement to her.

Interestingly, God doesn't strike Judah or Tamar dead. Instead, months later, Tamar gives birth to twins, and one of them, Perez, winds up in the genealogy of Jesus.

Daytime Drama

Anyone who says the Bible is boring is really saying, "I haven't read the Bible very much." This is some daytime drama. Or late-night talk-show material, the kind where the audience chants somebody's name, whether it's the host's, the guest's, or the security guard's. Why in the world is this crazy story in there?

Well, when God decided He was going to send His Son into the world, He knew He wanted to work through the lineage of Abraham and Sarah. They only had one son, so Isaac was a pretty obvious choice. But Isaac had two sons: Esau and Jacob. Which one to choose? God, for reasons all His own, chose Jacob.

Then Jacob complicated everything by having twelve sons. One of them was very famous, the namesake of a Broadway musical, in fact. Joseph would have been the obvious choice and made the most sense. We've logged many Sunday school hours learning about his great character—one of the few guys in the Old Testament who, once he got there, never really strayed too far off the right path. So if we'd done the choosing, we'd probably have gone with Joseph.

But the choice was God's, and He chose a different son—not the oldest, not the best, not even the favorite. God chose Judah, and that was scandalous. If His decision were made today, we'd politely say, "That's kind of random." You see, Judah's escapade with Tamar isn't the only thing we know about him. We also know that when his brothers got together to kill Joseph, it was Judah's idea to sell him into slavery—not because killing Joseph would have been wrong but because they wouldn't have gained much from doing so. Even back then he was cutting deals. Judah conspired with his brothers and lied to their father, telling him a wild animal tore his brother to shreds. He watched his father grieve while he pocketed the money and never said a word about it. He probably would have taken this secret to his grave—just as he'd planned to do with the "cult prostitute" who could not be found. You won't find Judah in Hebrews 11, where other heroes of the faith are listed. He's a terrible son, a terrible brother, and a terrible father.

We know that twenty years after his successful plan that sold Joseph out, Judah and nine of his brothers traveled to Egypt to buy food during a famine. If you know the story, you already know Joseph was in charge of all the food distribution there. Of course, they didn't recognize him—Joseph was young when they saw him last, and twenty years can change a person's appearance drastically. But Joseph certainly recognized them. And we know that Joseph eventually forgave his brothers and helped them. Based on what we know about Judah, had the sandal been on the other foot, it's not likely he would have acted as graciously.

So when I say it's "scandalous" or "random" for God to have selected Judah to be the line through which His Son would be sent, it's justifiable. But maybe that's the whole point. Judah never broke ranks; he never confessed, never came clean about his role in Joseph's disappearance. And as far as we can tell, he never even apologized. When Joseph finally had the upper hand, he blindsided Judah with grace. Judah got the exact opposite of what he deserved.

God chose Judah, yet Judah is bad. He deserves coal in his stocking. He deserves to be the one burned at the stake for selling his brother into slavery, lying to his parents, raising the kind of boys who would treat a woman like an object, going to a prostitute, sleeping with her in such a way so as to not even bother looking at her face long enough to recognize her as his own daughter-in-law! He should be a candidate for capital punishment; instead he's a candidate for grace.

Why? Because God wants people to know they can't come to Him on the basis of their own merits. You don't get into God's family because you deserve it, and your behavior can never disqualify you from it. Promising to change and do better does nothing to heal your past, does nothing about your secrets, and does nothing about the brokenness you've created in other people's lives. Your only hope is that someone else will come and do for you what you can't do for yourself, save you in your mess, and make your life story worth something.

That's what Joseph did for Judah; that's what God did for Judah. And that's precisely what God did for us. God, for reasons all His own, has always chosen the broken people, the messed-up people, the people with a past, the people with secrets, the people with damage. He sent His Son into this world to extend grace to people who didn't deserve it—even to those who, out of sheer rebellion or fear that they'd never be able to measure up, run from Him. Judah shows us that a relationship with God never begins with, "Here's what I promise to do differently." It always begins with, "Here's what has been done for me, and I can never repay it."

Eventually Judah and his brothers get their father Jacob to Egypt, too. When he's on his deathbed, he summons Judah and says, "Through your descendants will come a king, and your brothers' descendants will bow down to him." How did Jacob know?

Sure enough, generations later, from the line of Judah, a boy named David was born. Generations after that, from the same line, a boy named Jesus was born—because of Judah and because of all the Judahs in the world.

The Bridegroom of Blood

MOST EVERYONE IS familiar with the story about Moses and the burning bush. God appears to Moses in a bush that is on fire, but it doesn't burn up completely; it just continues burning. Then God calls Moses to Egypt (where he had been raised) to lead the Israelites out of slavery. Moses tries to talk his way out of it, but God persists. Moses finally relents.

Moses confronts the pharaoh, using his brother Aaron as his spokesman—God agreed to this arrangement—and demands that the people be allowed to leave. Pharaoh stubbornly refuses. Bring forth the plagues. And the Passover. And the parting of the Red Sea. Most of us probably picture it just as vibrantly Technicolor as Cecil B. Demille's version.

But there is one little episode that landed on the editing-room floor. Right there in the middle of Moses' return to Egypt, God tried to kill him.

This is crazy. They have a long conversation where God convinces Moses to go. Moses eventually agrees. He goes to tell his father-in-law, packs up the wife and kids, and heads out toward Egypt. And that's when God tries to kill him. Why? Why now? Why go through the whole argument at the burning bush if you're just planning on killing him? This does not seem to make sense.

Moses, his wife Zipporah, and their son are staying at the ancient Egyptian equivalent of a Motel 6 for the night when God comes at him. Now for whatever reason, Moses is not circumcised, and neither is his son. And that makes God mad—mad enough to kill.

Some say Moses must have had some sort of fit or seizure, but somehow Zipporah knew something bad was happening. And somehow she knew how to fix the problem.

She took out a knife and circumcised their son. Then she took the foreskin and touched Moses' private parts with it. Yes, his private parts. *Feet* is a Hebrew euphemism for private parts. Every Jewish person reading this story would know that she did not touch his feet. Zipporah calls Moses "a bridegroom of blood," and God decides to leave him alone. The end.

Foreskin, Foreshadowing

Ummmm . . . OK. Where shall we begin?

Zipporah is one tough lady. It takes something special to circumcise your son while God is trying to kill your husband. Namely, a steady hand.

Also, it should be noted that if you read the early chapters of the book of Exodus, women actually do all the saving there. I mean, yes, it's God, but He accomplishes His purposes through women (the two midwives, Moses' mother, his sister, Pharaoh's daughter, and now Moses' wife).

Anyone remember the name of the pharaoh during all of this? No, you do not because he is not named. And yet the Bible tells us that the two midwives are named Shiphrah and Puah.

Can we take a detour and be honest about something? Circumcision is crazy, and it's weird that we talk about it like it's no big deal. No one would come up with this idea on their own—trust me. But God told Abraham this was going to be a sign of the covenant between the two of them, and Abraham should continue the practice by passing it down to his son and his son's son, etc. I imagine Abraham must have felt ripped off (no pun intended) since Noah got a rainbow, but this was the identifying marker of a descendant of Abraham. There were hygienic reasons that we know about now, but back then, if they knew about that, they didn't mention it. It wasn't done out of concern for the boy's health; it was out of respect for the God of their forefathers Abraham, Isaac, and Jacob.

But Moses wasn't circumcised, and neither was his son. It's not too hard to understand why Moses wasn't. When he was born, the Egyptians were killing all the baby boys. The parents of those baby boys were probably trying to keep them quiet, hidden, and safe; circumcision probably worked against that. Plus, he was rescued by the Pharaoh's daughter and raised in the Pharaoh's household. It would have been hard to sneak a mohel in there to perform the surgery. This is the kind of thing that, if it doesn't get done when you're a baby, it probably isn't going to get done. Not everyone is as compliant as Father Abraham.

Zipporah circumcises her son and touches her husband "down there" with the bloody foreskin. This was a kind of vicarious circumcision, identifying her husband with the circumcision of her son. Maybe she didn't circumcise him because they had to get to Egypt, and traveling under those circumstances would have been painful.

At this point we should probably talk a little about why circumcision is such a big deal. Trust me, I don't want to talk about it anymore than you want to read about it, but we must. It's too weird not to understand it, and—like the act itself—we'll only need to do this once, and then we can all get back to our regular lives.

Before God tells Abraham to circumcise himself (Gen. 17), a covenant is made between the two of them (Gen. 15). We speak of entering into a covenant. Ancient people (and the Hebrew language) literally would speak of "cutting covenant." In this ceremony three animals are cut into pieces, and their parts are laid out in a symmetrical pattern with an aisle down the middle. Normally the weaker party of the two would walk through the animal pieces and swear loyalty to the stronger party. In essence, they would say, "If I fail in my loyalty to you, may I end up the same way these animals have ended up."

What makes the covenant between God and Abraham odd is that it's not Abraham who walks down the aisle; it's God. Even though He's the stronger party, God is the One who places Himself under a curse if He does not keep His word. Genesis 17 is Abraham's chance to match. By cutting off his foreskin, he is essentially saying, "May I and my offspring be cut off like this flap of skin if we do not act in loyalty to God."

Circumcision is a symbol of the costly grace of God. We cannot earn the covenant; it is a gift. But it demands our all; it is costly.

Still, we haven't figured out why God would try to kill Moses. That seems a little bit extreme to me. If God really wanted Moses dead, Moses would have been dead; there are enough stories scattered throughout the Bible of people who were struck dead in an instant. It's no big deal for God to kill a man; He's done it before.

Then let us add this: In a sense, doesn't God want to kill us all? Jesus did say that only those who are willing to lose their lives for His sake would find eternal life. He says we must deny ourselves, take up our cross, and follow Him—presumably to death (why else would we pick up an instrument of death like a cross?). The apostle Paul certainly knew this and wrote, "I have been crucified with Christ and I no longer live, but Christ lives in me. The life I now live in the body, I live by faith in the Son of God, who loved me and gave Himself for me" (Gal. 2:19b–20).

Dietrich Bonhoeffer said, "When Christ calls a man, he bids him come and die."[1] You can only enter the kingdom of God by dying a kind of death. So in that sense God seeks to kill us all for our own good. In the act of baptism, we identify with the death, burial, and resurrection of Jesus—knowing that if we die with Him we shall also live forever with Him.

Perhaps this is what God had in mind for Moses—not so much a physical death but a personal one. Moses had to die to any unhealthy notion of self so he could be brought back to life as the man God intended him to be. A man who has died and come back to life has very little to fear.

Notes

1. Dietrich Bonhoeffer, *The Cost of Discipleship* (New York: Touchstone, 1995).

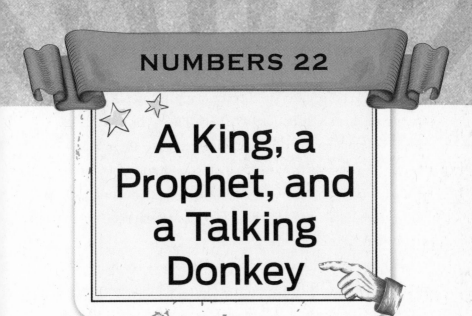

NUMBERS 22

A King, a Prophet, and a Talking Donkey

THERE'S A GUY in the book of Numbers named Balaam. He's a diviner, an oracle, a prophet for hire. He's the kind of guy people sought out to grant them blessings and to curse their enemies.

The Israelites are on the warpath, headed for the promised land, conquering everyone they meet. They've devastated two kings already: Sihon, king of the Amorites, and Og, king of Bashan. Operation Promised Land is going as planned. Meanwhile, back in Moab, the military might of the Israelites has gotten the attention of King Balak. He's concerned that his kingdom is next so he forms an alliance with the Midianites, figuring their combined strength might be enough to stave off these Hebrews. Then he remembers that odd guy who can throw blessings and curses around like horseshoes at the company picnic. A blessing from Balaam might be just what the doctor ordered. Also, the king wonders if he might just persuade the oracle to deliver a curse on the heads of those wandering Jews. So he sends emissaries from Moab and Midian with a trunkful of money for Balaam. Every man—even a messenger for the gods—has his price, right?

When the emissaries arrive, Balaam asks them to sleep over for a night while he consults God. The next morning he has good news and bad news. The good news is that he received an answer from God. The bad news is that God told him not to take them up on their offer, particularly the part about the cursing. Turned out God didn't want His messenger to curse His people. (Imagine that.)

Tails tucked between their legs, the emissaries return to Moab and report everything to the king. Balak assumes they simply haven't matched Balaam's price yet. He sends a second round of higher-level cabinet members with a promise of more riches than they could carry.

Balaam tells them he needs to consult with God, and they sleep over again. This time, however, in the morning he tells them that God will allow him to travel with them back to Moab. But he warns them that he is under strict orders to say only what God tells him to say. So off they go.

Balaam saddles up his trusty donkey, but something about all of this didn't sit right with God. God had told Balaam once already not to go. That should have been sufficient. He sends an angel to block the road, an angel Balaam could not see, an angel only Balaam's donkey could see. This, as you might suspect, was unsettling to the donkey.

The donkey jerks off the road and tears off through a field, a vineyard with walls on both sides. The angel is quicker than the donkey anticipates, though, and the angel shows up again in the path. The donkey tries to squeeze by, crushing Balaam's foot against the wall. Then, seeing that there is no way to get around the angel, the donkey gives up and lies down. When the going gets tough, the tough lie down in a field.

Now remember that Balaam can't see any of this. All he knows is that his donkey has gone crazy. Something has gone screwy here, and Balaam is determined to get back on the road and see just how much money may or may not be his depending on what he may or may not be allowed to say. Balaam nudges the donkey, then gently prods the donkey. Finally he beats the donkey, threatening to kill it! Clearly Balaam is not a member of PETA.

Now this is where the story takes a really strange turn. The donkey, as if this is the most normal thing in the world, looks at Balaam and speaks. "Why are you hitting me?"

(Helpful hint: even though the Bible says the donkey is a "she," I am conditioned to hear Eddie Murphy's voice when the donkey speaks in the story.)

Balaam, maybe because he's not thinking clearly after all the mayhem, answers back. "I hit you because you're making me look like a fool in front of my new friends. You're lucky I don't kill you!"

"I'm your donkey, right? The same one you ride all the time. Have I ever done anything like this before?"

"Well, no."

And then Balaam's eyes were opened to see what the donkey had seen all along. The angel explains that if the donkey hadn't diverted them from the path, he was all set to kill Balaam. The donkey saved Balaam's life.

Balaam apologizes and says he'll turn back and go home if that's what the angel wants. The angel says to continue, but remember: say only what God tells you to say. Balaam continues on his journey, probably being supercareful to give the donkey a little extra food and water, trying to think light thoughts on his ride. Once he arrives in Moab, the king uses everything he can think of to get Balaam to throw a curse at Israel. Balaam tries, but a blessing comes out instead. So they go to a new location and try again. And another blessing comes out. Maybe the third time would be the charm? Nope. Unless you're Israel. Balaam can only say what God tells him to say, and all He tells him is to bless Israel. Message received, loud and clear.

Hee-haw, Hee-haw

I once asked a friend to endorse a project I was working on. I wanted to do some marketing, and I needed several quotes from respectable people. My friend wrote back with this: "God spoke through a donkey in the Old Testament, and now it appears he's doing it again."

The king of Moab was nervous, and that's understandable. He can hear the sound of the Israelites marching, and he knows it's just a matter of time before they come at him. So he forms an alliance with Midian. Again that's completely understandable. Next he attempts to secure a blessing for his people and a curse on these invaders. I get it. The king is simply doing what comes naturally.

But Balaam refuses to cooperate. He can only do what God tells him. No amount of money could change that. This wasn't a negotiating ploy. Balaam was no training camp holdout looking to sign a max contract.

People with money often have a hard time understanding someone who is more interested in God's will than in their wealth. The king thought you could buy a blessing and a curse. I've tried to play Let's Make a Deal with God before. Haven't you?

"God, if you get me out of this mess, I will go on that mission trip over spring break."

"God, if you get me that promotion, I promise I will start tithing immediately."

"God, after all I've done for You, You at least owe me this."

It's kind of gross when you read it like that, but it's all too easy for us to start believing we can somehow pay God off or persuade Him to do what we want Him to do. But is that the kind of God you want? A God who can be bought and sold like that?

I don't think any of us wants a God who auctions off His blessings to the highest bidder—not really. And thankfully, that's not the God we find in the pages of the Bible.

We find, instead, a God who makes promises and keeps them—a God who understands that a promise stands immune to changing circumstances and inflation, a God who has no pressure point we can manipulate, a God who does not negotiate, a God who abides no backroom bribes, and a God who cannot be bargained with. When God makes a promise, it is guaranteed. Thank God for that. And He promises, "If you confess with your mouth, 'Jesus is Lord,' and believe in your heart that God raised Him from the dead, you will be saved" (Rom. 10:9).

Of course, plenty of folks have come along and added all sorts of stipulations and tests of orthodoxy, giving people the idea that the promise of God (salvation) can be bought with our good deeds. But according to God, a promise is a promise.

Jesus promises never to leave us or forsake us. Still we worry that choosing purity and holy living might leave us alone and excluded. But according to God, a promise is a promise.

God assures us that if we trust in Him and do what He asks, we can all but eliminate anxiety and temptation. And yet our lives remain filled with worry and sin. Rather than trusting God to keep His promises, we try to negotiate our agenda over His. We're not so different from King Balak, are we?

Then there's Balaam. Imagine being in his shoes. A foreign king offers you wealth and status. Not many people turn down an offer like that. And what if the king isn't really asking? What if the next time someone knocks on the door, it's not an emissary but an assassin? How do you say no to an offer you can't refuse?

God's people have never been strangers from trouble when a nation gets a mind to go to war. That was certainly the case for Christians in Germany when Hitler began introducing one atrocity after another. What were their options? Go along to get along? Withdrawal? Passive resistance?

Speaking truth to power has never been easy. Not for Bonhoeffer. Not for Martin Luther King Jr. Not for William Wilberforce. Not for Balaam. Not for Balaam's donkey.

From the moment Jesus was born, He was a threat to the powers of this world. King Herod dispatched soldiers to kill the baby boys in that area. Eventually both the religious and governmental powers conspired to murder the Savior on a cross. This is what happens when one man or woman chooses to follow the voice of God rather than acquiesce to the powerful and mighty.

God will not be seduced by power, and neither will His people. Yes, power is alluring, and we can convince ourselves that we will use it only for good. That's how Christians rationalized the Inquisition and the Crusades and the slave trade.

God will use whatever means He can to warn us. It is far too easy for us to stray from the path of God toward the path of power. If we need to be slammed into a wall by a talking donkey, so be it.

JOSHUA 2

Nicknames

GOD'S PEOPLE STAND at the door of the promised land, ready to take what is theirs. The plan is to do this city by city, gradually retaking the land God promised them. They cross the Jordan River and stare down at the city of Jericho. Joshua, their fearless leader, sends two men to Jericho on a reconnaissance mission; once they assessed the strengths and weaknesses, they would formulate a plan of attack. With so much riding on their intelligence, how did these two guys wind up in a brothel in Jericho?

Maybe they didn't mean to, or maybe they did. And it wouldn't be an isolated incident. According to the official report, they were sneaking their way through the city, spying around like all spies do, when they were spotted. The spotters go to the king and say, "We think there may be two Hebrew spies in the city." The king instructs to locate them.

By this time the sun is starting to set, and the two spies decide to hide someplace with a lot of traffic—someplace where it wouldn't be unusual for strangers to come and go, a place where anonymity and discretion are a priority. So they duck into a house of ill repute, which happens to be built into the city walls. When the cops show up, they knock on the door—a polite gesture, I guess; but Rahab's isn't the sort of place you barge into. Taking advantage of the cops' manners, Rahab sends the Hebrew spies to hide on the roof.

When questioned about her visitors, Rahab says, "Oh, you just missed them. You might be able to catch them if you hurry." After the authorities have cleared out, she goes upstairs and tells the spies, "I know your God has given this land to you." And the name she calls "God" is a rarely used word. It was the highest ranking word she could come up with—the most dignified and powerful name she could think of, *Elohim*. She identifies the Hebrew God as the God over all the other gods. She reveals that the entire city is terrified of them because they have already heard about the Red Sea and other miraculous victories. Remarking on the Hebrew God's power, she again identifies Him as God of both heaven and earth. Then she asks for a favor.

"I've done something kind for you. Would you do something kind for me? When you come to take this city, will you spare my family?" How could they refuse?

Rahab helps the spies escape with a rope through the window and instructs them on how to leave the city undetected. When they return to Joshua, they tell him how the entire city is scared to death and that taking the city would be way easier than they thought.

God's subsequent instructions sound more like a parade than a siege: "You won't even need your weapons for the first week—just a good pair of hiking boots. You're all just going to walk—not run, not menace, not strut, just walk—around the city walls. That's it. One day, one lap. Second day, another lap. Do this for a week. Then on the seventh day you'll walk seven laps and then shout. Any questions?" Yes—do we need floats or to throw candy?

Everyone does everything according to the plan, and on the seventh day—while the people are shouting their lungs out—the walls collapse on themselves. Did the collective noise and sound waves crash the walls? Did the collective footsteps shake the foundations? We do know it was a mighty demonstration of God's power through a unified people. And we also know that chaos and mayhem ensued.

The people in Jericho were already panicked; the crumbled walls just made matters worse. The Hebrews pretty much walk in untouched and take everything. And in the middle of all this chaos and terror, God reaches in and spares one family because of the faith of one Canaanite prostitute. And the story ends with its own little version of happily ever after: "And she lives in Israel to this day" (Josh. 6:25).

Name Game

Pop culture has given us lots of characters with nicknames: Conan the Barbarian, Dennis the Menace, Dora the Explorer. These nicknames give us some clue about the character and nature of the person: Conan is a barbarian; Dennis is a menace; and Dora loves to explore.

Rahab . . . well . . . Rahab was a prostitute—a harlot—and she had the nickname to prove it. No reason to be bashful about it. It's a matter of historical record. Nearly every time you read about her, you'll read her nickname. Granted, she stopped turning tricks at some point. Eventually, she settled down, got married, and had a baby. But she still had that nickname. And she knew the territory that came with her nickname. Men treated her as an object; women treated her as a threat. She knew contempt and what it felt like to be the punch line to a crude joke.

Jesus probably knew what that felt like, too; after all, His birth was rumored to be illegitimate. People would sometimes say, "We know who our father is. Do you, Jesus?"

What was Rahab feeling as she watched the Israelites march around her city? Did anyone look up to see that red cord dangling from her window, swaying there in the wind, marking a prostitute's house for salvation? If everyone else in town was terrified, what about her? Was she scared, too? Scared that it might not work or that they might forget? It wouldn't be the first time a man had promised her something and not come through.

Still the rope was never pulled back inside; it remained in place as she waited through the crazy tactics of these Jewish people. And they kept their promise—she was saved. She and her whole family lived among the Israelites from then on as an illustration of something we still have a hard time understanding: God will spare a foreigner, an outsider, an enemy, someone who by law should be killed.

But that's not the best part. Rahab didn't just live among the Israelites; she became one of them. One day she's minding her own business when a man named Salmon asks her to have dinner, or coffee, or something. Maybe he was one of the two spies—we don't know. We do know that she says yes, and one thing leads to another—first comes love, then comes marriage, and then comes little Boaz in a baby carriage. Boaz grows up and marries an outsider from Moab, a woman named Ruth. They have a baby, and their great-grandson turns out to be King David.

And you know what that means. It means that a pagan prostitute from Jericho is in the lineage of Jesus. I know that because a guy named Matthew wrote it all down.

Incidentally, Matthew had a nickname of his own: Matthew the tax collector. He had surely heard his share of jokes at his expense. He certainly knew what it felt like to be an outsider. Maybe that's why, when Matthew writes her name, he does not include her nickname.

I know what it's like to have a past, and I probably earned a nickname or two in my life. Maybe you have, too. Maybe you did things you regret. Maybe you're so ashamed of your past life that you can't walk into a church building without feeling like damaged goods.

You are not an intruder to any place where the gospel is preached; you belong there. God has called you there, and if the people in that room don't want you, go find another room where the true gospel is preached. A church is not only a sanctuary for thieves, murderers, and prostitutes but also a hospital where they can find healing.

You see, the blood of Jesus was shed for the grossest of sins, including the ones we have made socially acceptable, like greed, pride, gluttony, and self-righteousness. In the church all those who have been outcasts are received and treated as the children of God that they are. New life begins, healing happens, and the Abba Father (one of His nicknames) of both heaven and earth shows Himself to be compassionate beyond belief.

Holy War and the Old Testament

GOD PROMISES AN old man a child. It takes a while, but it happens. The old man and his old wife have a baby. It's a miracle and everyone lives happily ever after. But the baby wasn't the only thing the old man was promised; he was also promised a place to live, a place where his children and his children's children would live—a land where his descendants would live forever. When it's just one family, that land doesn't have to be very big—maybe just a few acres, tops. As that family grows, however, finding a place to put everyone can become problematic.

Oh, the old man was also told that eventually his family would be more numerous than the stars in the desert sky. Real estate can really become an issue by then; so, where is this promised land? We know it as Israel. And, again, when it was just Abraham and his extended family, they didn't take up too much room.

By the time we get to Moses, however, there are probably more than two million of them. They need some space. Of course, there is a problem—and I'm not just talking about acreage. The real problem is that, by the time we get to Moses, the people haven't lived in their promised land for more than four hundred years. They get back to their home, and someone else is living there. Four centuries is a long time to expect your land to be allowed to sit vacant. So, what do you do when you come back from nearly half a millennium of slavery to find someone squatting on your land? God said, "Kill them." Wait . . . what?

You read that right. God said to kill them all—every man, woman, child, animal—anything of theirs that breathed. Seems a little . . . um, much. It sounds like God is advocating genocide. This is unthinkable, isn't it? It's hard to believe.

It would appear that the Israelites found it hard to believe, too. After all, they failed to follow through on it. Sometimes they obeyed; sometimes, though, they balked. And when they did, when they failed to do precisely what God told them to do and instead spared the lives of the people inhabiting their promised land, it came back to haunt them.

Mirror, Mirror

OK, this story is crazy for obvious reasons. And you don't hear many preachers doing a neat and tidy five-part series on the conquest of the promised land. When you do hear people talk about this, they tend to overspiritualize it. You know what I mean; they read passages about battles and then talk about how it means that God will strengthen you against fear, or cancer, or some other obstacle like that. Of course, that's true, but that's not what this story means at all.

When you read the Bible, you have to start with what the Bible literally says. These were literal battles, with literal people who literally died. Now you can learn a lot about a person by which character they identify with in a particular story. Take, for example, the parable of the prodigal son. If you relate to the younger son, we learn something about you; if, however, you relate more to the older brother, we learn something different. If you feel more like the father, we learn something different again.

Or take the parable of the vineyard workers. The boss hires some people early in the day and some people late in the day; in the end they both make the same amount. I know a lot of people who relate more with those who worked all day and feel like, maybe, they got cheated or those latecomers shouldn't get paid as much. When we honestly connect with a particular character—that is, see ourselves, including our shortcomings and reactions—this reveals a lot about ourselves.

So back to this business about genocide in the promised land. Our self-serving bias is revealed when we rush too quickly to identify ourselves with God's chosen people. This is, after all, what makes the story hard to swallow, isn't it? We can't imagine God telling us to go and kill an entire race of people. This is especially difficult to reconcile with our views regarding the sanctity of life; certainly, there were at least a few pregnant women living in those Canaanite cities. God told His people to kill everything—including those unborn babies. This is problematic for us.

But what if we're *not* supposed to identify with the chosen people? What if, in fact, we are supposed to think of ourselves as Canaanites? Occupying a land that wasn't given to us in the first place? Interlopers? People who deserve death? Go share your views on this story with a member of the Cherokee nation and then explain to him how you think America has always been a Christian nation.

This story's not just crazy; it's a stumbling block. In the second century there was a man named Marcion. He read this story among others and said there's an irreconcilable gap between the loving God of the New Testament and the vengeful, violent God of the Old Testament. He suggested we just cut out the Old Testament altogether. I hope you know that's not the right approach. If we find some discrepancy between God as He is revealed in the Old Testament and God as He is revealed in the New Testament, the problem isn't with the Bible; the problem must be with how we're reading it!

So what gives? What's with this story about God demanding that His people kill others? First, we should note one thing: there is no such thing as "holy war" in the Bible. War is never holy; violence is never holy. Violence is upsetting to God; it's one of the reasons He sends the flood, to purge the earth of its violence. Violence is a result of the fall (as opposed to many other religions of the time, where the gods were inherently violent), and, as such, it was not part of the original intent, nor will it be part of the restored kingdom of God. Is it sometimes necessary in a fallen world because of the hardness of people's hearts? Yes. Does it ever bring God joy to slaughter people? No.

War is like polygamy, slavery, and divorce. It exists in the Bible because it existed in the world due to the sinfulness of the human race. God has always come to people just as they are; He started there and gradually formed us into what we were originally designed to be. It always takes time to teach someone a better way, especially when God is not simply dealing with an individual but all of humanity. But in the process sin and evil must be dealt with.

In the story of Noah and the flood, God eradicates the violence Himself. In this story God enlists the assistance of His people. He promises them that He'll do all the hard work (provided they walk in obedience), and they'll only have to do some mop-up work. This was the case with Jericho—God made the walls fall down, and not one Israelite was harmed in the battle.

But let's not rush too quickly past this idea of God dealing with sin and evil. It's hard for us to imagine, but the evil present among the Canaanites was so bad, it was as if an entire society had gone past the point of no return. God had given them plenty of time to mend their evil ways, but they had just gotten worse. They practiced human sacrifice; prostitution was a form of worship. Imagine finding out your wife was pregnant, watching her deliver you a son, taking that child and offering him as a burnt sacrifice—laying him on the altar while he is still alive and wiggling. Or suppose it is a girl; you know that one day she may very well be called into service as a prostitute for your god.

Now think of what that does to a culture. Multiply it one child after another, generation after generation. Think of doing this in the name of your god, and think how that affects the children who survive and are brought up in such a society. This is what it means for a people to reach the full measure of sin. God says it has to be stopped.

For reasons of His own—and reasons He has chosen not to share—God never abolishes evil altogether from this world. I cannot understand this, but I am told repeatedly that God will contain evil and restrain evil. God will keep evil in check and prevent it from doing its worst. Perhaps the thing I find most unsettling is the fact that, while the children of Israel are the instruments God uses to rid the world of the evil practices of the Canaanites, the children of Israel are also part of the problem. They're supposed to bring justice to the world, but it's not like they're standing on some pristine patch of moral high ground. They fail again and again, and God must rescue them from scrape after scrape. This is the consistent story of the messy ways in which God must work to bring the world out of the mess it has created for itself. And there is always a sense that the plan isn't quite working out the way it should, that the only way forward is to hold these amazing promises in one hand and the reality of disaster in the other, remembering that God, somehow, remains sovereign over it all the whole time. In the end we never get the kind of picture we want. We want a world with everything explained in a neat and tidy way; that explanation never fully comes. We want the universe to be a machine, and we want God to be the sort of mechanic who can keep it all in good working order.

What we get, instead, is a story—a mysterious one, at that—in which God attempts to pursue justice in an otherwise unjust world. Rather than scrapping the existing characters and playing space, God has to redeem everything by acting from within the framework He established in the beginning. To do this, God must work with things as they are—at least, to begin with. Everything is shot through with ambiguity and inconsistency; there is no one who wears a purely black hat or a purely white one . . . not until much, much later.

The Sun Stood Still

THE ISRAELITES SPENT forty years wandering around the wilderness. Moses died, and Joshua takes over the leadership role. They stand ready to cross over the Jordan River and move into their promised land. But there is one little problem: The land is occupied. There are people living there—lots of them—and they're not really that excited about handing everything over to the Israelites and finding somewhere else to live, just because these wandering Jews believe their God told them they could have it. I say it's a little problem, though, because God isn't afraid to kill people who won't cooperate.

Word of this had spread far and wide. Anyone who dared attack the Israelites ended up defeated. First Heshbon.

Then Bashan. Then Ashtaroth. Now they crossed the Jordan River and Jericho fell—literally. Israel did hit one bump in the road; Ai beat them back, but it was just a temporary setback brought about by a bad egg named Achan. He had stolen some stuff, and God used Ai to prove a point about purity and honesty. Once that got straightened out, Ai was destroyed like the others. So everyone was terrified of the Israelites, and they all decided to band together thinking their united force could withstand and repel the Israelites. Every nation, that is, but Gibeon.

The Gibeonites were just as scared as everyone else, but they had a different plan. They found some old moldy bread, put on their most worn-out clothes, and dirtied themselves up. Then they approached the Israelites, telling them a sad and untrue story.

"We're not from around here," they said, "but we've heard all the amazing things this God of yours has done. You have defeated everyone you've encountered. We've come all this way because we don't want any trouble. We'd like to sign a peace treaty with you."

It certainly looked like they were telling the truth. The journey must have been long since the bread was probably fresh when they left, and their clothes have been torn up by all the travel. "We'll do it!" said the Israelites.

One problem here: they forgot to check with God first. God would have told them the people were lying. The

Israelites signed the treaty; three days later they figured out that they had been tricked. Israel wanted to get back at them, but they had made a promise, and a promise is a promise.

The Israelites weren't the only ones angry with the Gibeonites; the people from the other cities were a little upset as well. They were already afraid of trying to fight the Israelites. Now they would have to take on the Gibeonites, too! So they waited for the Israelites to get far enough away from Gibeon, and then they attacked! The Gibeonites, of course, sent word to the Israelites, saying, "Help! Come save us!" I wonder if Israel considered taking the scenic route to get there.

Understandably, Joshua was reluctant to trust them this time. Fool me once, shame on you. Fool me twice, shame on me. So he consulted God, and God told them to go ahead and fight. They marched nearly thirty miles through the night and took the attacking armies by surprise early in the morning. A chase ensued; God sent a hailstorm to slow them down. Think of that: God literally threw ice cubes at them! The Bible says the chunks of ice killed more people than the Israelite soldiers did! Oh, and not one of the Israelites gets pelted.

The day progressed, and Joshua started to worry that the enemy might get away during the night. If they succeeded, they might regroup and rally the next day. So Joshua prays this prayer: "Sun, stand still over Gibeon, and moon, over the Valley of Aijalon" (Josh. 10:12).

And that's when the story really gets crazy. The sun stood still; the earth stopped rotating. Or maybe there was an eclipse? Or a mirage? Something shifted out there that day.

God gave Joshua enough time to defeat five armies in one (albeit long) day. He'd never done anything like that before, and He never did anything like that again.

And the World Spins Madly On . . . or Not

Can we just get something out of the way first? I agree with those who say that a God who can pelt one side with hailstones and keep the other side free from harm, a God who can part the Red Sea and the Jordan River, a God who can provide manna in the wilderness and create everything there is . . . that God can probably figure out how to stop the rotation of the earth without having us all fly off into outer space or being drowned by the tidal waves that we might think would be inevitable. Yes, I agree.

I also think that's not a good enough answer—especially if you have a non-Christian friend who reads a story like this and says, "What is up with that?" I do think it's dumb for people to use this to say that people in the Bible are dumb and people who believe in the Bible are antiscientific. Just because it says the sun stood still doesn't mean as much as some people want to think it does. After all, in all our glorious enlightenment, we still refer to sunrise and sunset, even though we know the sun does not rise or set.

Truth is we don't know what happened. I have read everything I can find on this subject, and I don't have strong convictions one way or another. Maybe it was a poetic description of what happened; maybe it just seemed like the day slowed down. Maybe the earth's rotation actually slowed down or stopped. There are all sorts of stories to "prove" that this actually happened. I've read that there are accounts in Chinese, South American, and Egyptian histories. I haven't found an original source, so I'm inclined to think those are Christian urban legends. I also heard about a professor at Harvard or Yale who discovered some astronomical anomaly suggesting the earth is missing a day. Again, there are no reputable original sources of this story—at least none I can find. But what if it really *did* happen? Would that be so strange? Would it be unlike God to do something like that?

It is interesting that none of the other battles in Joshua are won with supernatural help like this—only Jericho and Gibeon. From here on out, they won their battles the old-fashioned way. That seems like exactly the kind of thing God might do—flex His muscles a little at the beginning to reassure His children that He's in control and strong enough to take care of them if and when they get into trouble. Then let them fight their own battles.

While we can't explain exactly what happened, I confess I probably would have laughed and made fun of Joshua for praying such a ridiculous prayer. I would have quickly said, "Sure, God could stop the sun for you, but really He probably won't do anything of the kind!" Just like I know God can heal cancer; I just don't think He does very often. Just like I know God can break through someone's hard heart; I just don't think He does very often.

I do love how matter of fact the Bible is about this story, though, beginning in verse 13, where it basically tells us, "Oh, and by the way, the earth completely stopped rotating so there would be enough time for Joshua to accomplish his task. As far as we know, there's never been another day like that one, before or since.".

While I'm pretty certain what my attitude would have been, this is also one of those things about which I would love to have been proven wrong. I love for God to show up bigger than I think He can. I would love to see Him cure more people of cancer, fix more marriages, soften more hard hearts, and do all those sorts of things we rarely see happen. And I also wish I prayed for those sorts of things more. It would make me laugh, cry, and clap my hands . . . and possibly become a better man.

Yes, I want to pray for big things like that to happen in my life. I wish I weren't so afraid to ask. How about you?

The Left-Handed Ways of God

AFTER MOSES DIED, Joshua succeeded in leading the people to take possession of their promised land. After Joshua died, however, the nation didn't really have a leader or a centralized government; they were more like a loose confederation of tribes. What ended up happening in Israel was simple: everyone just did whatever was right in his or her own eyes. Sadly this also meant they frequently disobeyed God.

It's important to note that they didn't really *forget* God or God's laws; they simply ignored the inconvenient bits. They cut some corners, compromised a little bit here and there, until it added up to a big, steaming pile of disobedience.

God has a better memory than any of us, and He has His ways of setting things straight. During this period of history, His preferred method was to send an invading horde of enemies from one of the surrounding nations. Every few decades God would use one of those groups to discipline a straying Israel. The people would recognize the error of their ways and cry out to God for deliverance. God would, in turn, raise up a leader—a judge—who would bail them out. One of the earliest judges was a man named Ehud, and his story is a crazy story.

Ehud was from the tribe of Benjamin—which means "son of the right hand"—which is ironic since a lot of the folks from the tribe of Benjamin turned out to be left-handed (cf., Judg. 20:16 and 1 Chron. 12:1). Ehud wasn't just left-handed, however; the Bible says he could not use his right hand. The implication is that something had happened to his right hand. Maybe he'd been injured. Or maybe he was born with some defect. Whatever it was, it was most likely visible. Hang on to that tidbit; that's an important part of the story.

Israel had rebelled against God, and God was disciplining them. They had been oppressed for eighteen years by the morbidly obese king of Moab, Eglon. Eglon should never have even been born, and the Moabites should never have existed. They were the product of the unholy union of Lot and one of his daughters.

But there he was, King Eglon, fat and mean to boot. And every year the Israelites had to present Eglon with a tribute—usually money, gold, or jewels—as protection money. Ehud volunteers to present the tribute because he wants to get physically close to Eglon.

He straps a short sword to his right thigh, to draw it with his left hand. Anyone expecting an attack would have expected it to come from the other side. But when they see Ehud, they figure he's no threat—after all, look at his poor right hand. He's disabled. No need to pat him down. Eglon never saw it coming.

Ehud presents the tribute and starts to leave. Then, sending everyone on ahead, he tells the king, "I have a secret message for you." The king beckons him close. Ehud draws the sword and plunges it into that giant belly. The sword sinks into his stomach right up to the handle, and—here comes the gross, crazy part—his fat closes over it. It's like his belly swallows the whole sword. And then he, er, relieves himself. I'm not making this up—read for yourself.

Eglon leaves and on his way out tells the king's attendants not to enter, explaining the king's need for, uh, "restroom privacy." Which wasn't completely a lie. Eventually they break down the door to the king's private chambers and make the gross discovery. They sound the alarm, but it's too late. Ehud has escaped and mobilized an army. The Moabites are defeated; Israel is liberated. The end.

Jesus Is Not Jeeves

I don't remember there being any Sunday school songs about this one, no "The Lord said to Ehud, 'I want you to stabby, stabby,'" or "King Eglon was a very fat man, and a very fat man was he." The memory verse is never from Judges 3; and, come to think of it, I have never heard a sermon about this whole episode, either.

But we can learn an important lesson from Ehud that will set the table for the rest of this book: God rarely does what we expect. And by *rarely*, I mean, almost never. God is, without a doubt, the most frustrating Being I have ever met in my life. I used to have this idea that following God would get easier as I got older; I could not have been more wrong. Secretly I thought that one day Jesus would flag me down while I was driving my car. He would tell me to scoot over, and he would take over driving. While Jeeves, I mean Jesus, chauffeured, I would sit back in the passenger seat and wave at all my friends as we drove past, enjoying the scenery. Jesus could make all the driving decisions, as long as He was steering me home. Admittedly, I'm a bit of a control freak, and it might take a while to adjust to not being in control. But Jesus would drive me wherever He wanted me to go, and I would learn to live with it.

I've learned as I get older that Jesus asks me to do something far more difficult than let Him drive; He flags down my car and says, "Follow Me." Then He goes to get in His own car. He has not given me good directions (and sometimes no directions). He's not really interested in giving me guidance; He wants to be my Guide.

Now some people are easy to follow. They drive the speed limit, slow down at intersections, use their turn signals, and brake early. Jesus is not like that; He blows through intersections and makes kamikaze lane changes. He may even try a left-hand turn from the right-hand lane. Following Jesus is not relaxing. It's the most exhausting, nerve-wracking, nail-biting experience imaginable. But this is what we are called to do—follow Him. I don't have much of a map. I have a vague, general idea of where I'm going, but mostly I'm just trying to stay as close to His back bumper as I can. And when I finally get where I'm going, I'll know I couldn't have done this on my own. The only way I'll get where I need to go is by paying attention to the Man in front of me.

That's what following Jesus means, and we're to stay on high alert because He could make a hard right at any moment. He doesn't always feel the need to use His turn signals. We may have to run a few yellow lights to keep up. We may have to make a U-turn and find Him again. But that's following Jesus; there's not really a pattern to it.

The plan of God often seems like it comes out of left field. Any relationship with God, any attempt to study His character and nature, will and should confound our expectations. This is the left-handed way of God. It's not the priest who saves the wounded man; it's the dirty Samaritan. It's not the oldest or the tallest who becomes the king; David was the runt of the litter. The chosen people are named after a heel-grabbing con man and trickster. The disciples aren't the best and brightest; most were uneducated, blue-collar, working-class stiffs, a tax agent, and one of them even has ties to a terrorist organization. Jesus does not save us through military victory but through suffering death on a cross.

Throughout the Bible, you will find God doing the unexpected. He uses the guy whose right hand is withered. The last are first. The servant of all is the greatest of all. The smart look dumb, and the foolish become wise. The proud are humbled, and the humble are exalted. Heroes are shown to be embarrassingly human. Enemy number one of the church ends up being its greatest evangelist. Honestly, my whole idea behind this book was to find the crazy stories in the Bible and show what they reveal about our amazingly sane God. But now I've come to realize that the entire Bible is crazy. It's not as if there are a few crazy stories tucked away in unusual corners of the text; they're everywhere.

This is our God. His character is as consistent as His behavior is erratic. His promise is as dependable as His plan is unpredictable. Sometimes, it is ten plagues; sometimes, it is Ten Commandments, or the death of the firstborn, or a virgin birth. Ultimately, it is an execution that leads to a resurrection. About the only sure thing in any of these stories is that there will always, always, always be a surprise.

JUDGES 11

Even When It Hurts

JEPHTHAH WAS BORN out of wedlock. His mother was a harlot. I can only imagine the names he got called when he was growing up. People said the same about Jesus. They teased Him and said, "Hey, we know who our father is. Do you?" That had to hurt—both of them. Jephthah knew his father, and his father took responsibility for him; but his stepbrothers threw him out when they got old enough. Jephthah ran to the land of Tob and joined a gang there and eventually, it seems, became their leader.

Like a lot of children born in less than ideal circumstances, Jephthah may have grown up feeling like he had to prove something. So, when the Ammonites picked a fight with the folks back in his hometown, the elders of Gilead took a road trip to Tob and begged him to come home and take command of the situation. Well, this was after no one would volunteer; Jephthah was their only hope. That's got to be at least a little bit vindicating, right? "Oh, aren't you the guys who ran me out of town before? And now you're crawling back to me begging me to come rescue you? OK, . . . let me think about it." This may have been his chance to prove he deserved a seat at the "legit" table; we don't know. For whatever reason, however, Jephthah decides to return to his homeland and stand up to the Ammonite bullies. He does so on one condition: being a pretty good student of history, he knows the whole effort will be futile unless God is with him. This was good information, but what Jephthah does with his knowledge is rash and foolish. Sadly, this is what he is now best known for.

He makes a foolish vow to the Lord: "If You will hand over the Ammonites to me, whatever comes out of the doors of my house to greet me when I return in peace from the Ammonites will belong to the LORD, and I will offer it as a burnt offering" (Judg. 11:30–31). Did he think it was going to be his beloved dog? A chicken? What in the world could he have been thinking? He fights the Ammonites. The Lord hands them over to him. He defeats twenty of their cities, and, when he went home, there was his daughter, coming out to meet him with singing and dancing! She was his only child, old enough to know what was going on, young enough to be unmarried. He wept. He tore his clothes. He was beside himself with grief. And he killed her and offered her as a burnt offering. He served as a judge in Israel for six years afterward and is considered a hero of the faith.

What the Heck

This is a crazy story. It makes me mad, sad, and confused all at the same time. The book of Judges is confusing; frankly, it's amazing it made it past the editors. In the book of Judges you read about God's people, leaders nonetheless, who plunge a dagger into the belly of a man, drive a tent peg through another man's head, use a millstone to crush yet another man's skull, and cut a woman into twelve pieces after she has died. If someone today were to write a book like this, I doubt many Christian bookstores would carry it. Yet these characters are considered heroes, which can make you wonder what the Bible's definition of *hero* is.

Still, each of the judges reveals something about God's character. We saw how Ehud shows us God's "left-handed" ways. Deborah was the unlikely judge, just as Jesus was the unlikely Messiah. Samson's death liberated God's people from their enemies—just like Jesus'. Gideon shows us that God's strength is perfected in our weakness. What in the world can we learn about God from Jephthah?

A man who would make such a vow should not be considered any kind of hero, and a man who would follow through on such a vow should be considered a criminal. He should have known better. But he didn't. And that may be the point: He didn't know better. His upbringing wasn't good; his family probably was not churchgoing. He probably didn't spend a lot of time around the dinner table going over the finer points of Leviticus. If he had, he would have known that God made a provision in case something like this should ever happen (seriously, check out Lev. 27:1–8).

Jephthah's mother was a prostitute, which means his father went to a prostitute at least once. Then his father allowed his other sons to chase Jephthah away. This is probably not a guy who led family devotionals. Just reading Judges gives me the impression that there weren't many people familiar with the Law of Moses.

Jephthah was foolish. The story is shocking, and it is supposed to be. Jephthah was faced with a difficult situation. Because of his rash vow, he had to choose which of two laws he should keep. The law forbade human sacrifice. The law demanded you keep your oaths—particularly the ones you make to God. Jephthah chose to keep his word and kill his daughter.

By the way, there's no use trying to explain this away as some attempt to do. If we are going to take the text seriously at all, we must allow the text to mean what it plainly means.

He killed his daughter and offered her as a burnt offering. Nowhere does the text say this pleased the Lord; we may infer that it did not. We may go so far as to draw the conclusion that YHWH would have preferred Jephthah to withdraw his vow, break his promise, and preserve human life. Could God have intervened here, as He did with Abraham and Isaac? Of course He could have, but during this time in history, God is teaching Israel to stand on its own, to learn how to make wise choices. God doesn't have to speak directly into each and every moral dilemma, particularly when He has spoken forcefully about the issue in the past. Jephthah's poor decision has terrible consequences, and consequences are often life's greatest teachers.

Still, I maintain we can learn something about God from Jephthah, and I believe it is this: God keeps His vows. The degree to which we are shocked by Jephthah's actions may not merely tell us how much we value human life and women in our society; it may also reveal a bit about how lightly we take vows today.

I'll admit that if I'd been in Jephthah's position, I would not have thought twice about breaking my vow to God. I could have easily rationalized it away. I know all the theological maneuverings, philosophical vindications, and psychological justifications for why I could obviously not do what I had promised God I would do. By the time I was done making my case, you might agree with me. You might even agree with me before I started making my case. We would both say it is because we value the life of that child so much, but we would both also know that we don't value our word very much at all these days.

Words matter. God takes words seriously, starting with His own. God said sin would equal death, and He meant it. God promised Israel the land where Jephthah grew up, and He meant it. God promised to deliver His people from their enemies, and He meant it. God promised to send His Son to earth to die for our sins, and He meant it. God promises us that one day everything that is currently upside down will get turned right-side up—that everything broken will get fixed, that everything sad will come untrue, and He meant that, too.

There were a couple of ways Jephthah could have spared his daughter. He could have paid a ransom; he could have refused to kill her and simply allowed God's curse to come upon him. He didn't. When our lives were on the line, our heavenly Father chose not to spare His own Son, sending Him instead to pay a ransom. Jesus refused to allow us to die, choosing instead to let God's curse come upon Him.

Jephthah made a terrible choice, and I bet he'd change a few things if given the opportunity. Thankfully, when Jesus made a difficult choice, we can trust He'd do it again if He had to.

JUDGES 19

No Good Guy in Sight

GOD HAD GIVEN His people a choice to obey Him or not. If they did, they would receive unbelievable blessings. If they did not, they would endure unbelievable consequences. It's the biggest no-brainer in the history of earth, but even today we still don't seem to get it.

As soon as Joshua and the people of his generation died, the next generation turned into a dumpster fire. They completely abandoned God and chose to worship other gods. So God got angry and punished them. The people suffered for years before asking God to help them. God raised up a judge to help them defeat their enemy and return them to a proper relationship with God . . . which doesn't last very long. Lather. Rinse. Repeat.

So goes the book of Judges, and it contains one haunting refrain that gets repeated every time they sink to a new low: "In those days there was no king in Israel; all the people did what was right in their own eyes." It's easy to think this is just a cycle, but it's not. It's a spiral. It's a downward spiral. Each time they rebel, they get worse. And by far the worst of the worst is what happens right at the end of the book.

A Levite—supposedly, a man of God—has a mistress whom he treats like an additional wife. Something happens—maybe she cheats on him, or gets angry at him, or something—and she decides to move back home to live with her parents. A few months go by, and the Levite shows up at their house. He's got a little speech he wants to deliver—tender words aimed at her heart.

Her father is excited to see him; maybe he wants his daughter to move out of the house so he can have his man cave back. He invites the Levite to stay and hang out for a while. They eat, drink, talk . . . and, after several days of this, the Levite and his "wife" leave.

Late in the afternoon they realize they need to find a place to stay the night. They approach a Canaanite city, but the Levite doesn't want to stay there; he thinks they'll be safer among their own kind, so they push on to a city called Gibeah—where the tribe of Benjamin lives. They don't know a soul there, but they're sure that the people will offer them hospitality. He is, after all, a man of God.

No such luck. They sit there in the town square look-ing lost until an old man spots them. "You folks can't stay out here all night. Come to my house," he says. Now there's something about the way he says it that leads us to believe something is off in this place, and it's not as safe as the Levite thought. By now one can no longer assume the people of Israel are automatically more moral than the Canaanites around them.

Later that night there's a knock on the door. Some of the lowlifes in town demanded that the host bring out his guest. They wanted to "sample his goods," so to speak. The host refuses, offering his virgin daughter and the Levite's concubine instead. The men insist. The Levite grabs his "wife" and shoves her out the door. She is gang-raped all night long. As the early light began to dawn, she manages to crawl to the entrance of the house where her husband was staying. She collapses there at the front door, unable to move any farther. The only words he ever speaks to her in this story come when he opens the door to find her body there. Four words: "Get up. Let's go."

She does not respond, so he picks her up, puts her on his donkey, and heads home. When he gets home, he takes a knife and cuts her body into twelve pieces, mailing them to each of the twelve tribes of Israel. This is a whole new level of gross. Was she dead when he found her? Did she die en route? Did he kill her? We are not told, but eleven of the tribes demand an explanation. He gives them his version of the story, and let's just say he spins it a little to make himself look better. And he misses the central point that people were cruel to his mistress, focusing on the threat the men of Gibeah made against him.

So the eleven tribes assemble and go to war against Benjamin. They take one man's word instead of insisting on two witnesses as the law demanded, and they decide to eradicate the tribe of Benjamin. They kill everything—men, women, children, even the animals. Only six hundred men manage to escape.

One man told one story about the rape of one woman, and it resulted in the death of twenty-five thousand men in one day. And that was after the men of Benjamin had killed forty thousand men from the other tribes. Think of it— sixty-five thousand soldiers died. Who knows how many died as "collateral damage"? All of that because a cowardly clergyman threw his mistress to the wolves.

But there was more. The eleven tribes realized they might have overreacted. Actually, they blame God for allowing this whole thing to happen, and then they try to undo the damage. These six hundred guys will need wives, but they've all made a pact that they would never allow one of their daughters to marry one of those men. How can they preserve their honor and still help the veterans of Benjamin?

They find one town that had not joined forces with them, and they remember saying that anyone who didn't join them deserved death. They march on that one town and kill everyone, except for the single ladies, who are captured and forced to marry the Benjaminite soldiers. Problem solved.

Except there were only four hundred virgins there. This is getting complicated! What should we do with the two hundred guys who lose the virgin lottery? Hmmm . . . well, what about Shiloh? They have that annual Virgin's Ball! Let the guys go there and kidnap wives from Shiloh. What a neat and tidy ending to this crazy story! The end.

Don't Miss the Irony

OK, just to be clear: they thought the solution to a problem created by men forcibly taking advantage of a woman was to let men forcibly take advantage of women. Right. That's crazy.

Some stories are crazy in a comic way, like a talking donkey. Other stories are crazy in a gross way, like Lot and his daughters. Still other stories are crazy in a depraved way that haunts your sleep. That's this story.

And obviously, this story doesn't get a lot of play in churches. Your children's ministry will not be reenacting this for VBS anytime soon. At least let's hope not.

So let's start the unpacking by asking where we can fix the blame for this horrifying story. The woman? She probably shouldn't have left the guy in the first place, but I'm not sure I can blame her—especially if this guy was abusive in the past. It's rare that the first case of abuse would involve cutting someone up into twelve pieces. So what about her father? Maybe he was afraid of the guy, too. Maybe he just wanted her out because daughters can be expensive. Then there's the host in Gibeah. He should have taken better care of his guests. Hospitality was a big deal for that culture, and she deserved his protection as much as the Levite did. But I'm sure he was scared of that mob.

The town of Gibeah should never have allowed such a situation to occur. There was obviously a complete breakdown of law and order in that place. The mob itself was obviously guilty. Sadly, we don't know if any of the men who committed the original crime may have been among the six hundred survivors. The eleven tribes of Israel were also guilty; they didn't conduct a very thorough investigation. They overreacted. Then they overcorrected. The Levite, too, was obviously a very bad man. He used his mistress for his own selfish needs, treating her like an object. He does not offer her any respect or dignity, no freedom of choice, no rights. He sleeps through her ordeal, showing no signs of remorse or sympathy. In light of his behavior, I'm not as surprised that he cut her up into pieces. He treated her with no love or respect. And lest any doubt remains of his true nature, when he offers his version of the story, he reveals just how self-centered he is. His shock is not over what they did to her but over what they meant to do to him.

This is a terrible story, and there's not really a good guy in sight. That's probably why we rarely discuss it. But there is another story we know well, and if we are careful, we might find some echoes of that story in this one.

It begins with a woman on a donkey and leads to a dead body, torn to shreds after having been abused all night. It also begs the question about whom to blame. Of course, the woman is Mary. The body is Jesus'. And we are the guilty ones.

Both stories reveal what humans become, how dark and depraved we are when there is no king and we all determine to do whatever is right in our own eyes. Thankfully, the second story finds hope and redemption where the first does not. In the second story the victim speaks, "Father, forgive them, because they do not know what they are doing" (Luke 23:34).

The mob didn't know. The eleven tribes didn't know. The Levite didn't know. And neither do we. We all fail to realize that whatever we do for the least of these, we do to Him. But God knows. God sees. God forgives and redeems and restores.

BOOK OF RUTH

Meat and Potatoes

GOD PROMISED ABRAHAM that his descendants would bless the rest of the world. Sometimes they blessed the world because of their behavior; other times they blessed the world in spite of their behavior. God blessed the world through them, even when He couldn't get them to cooperate with Him. God is not easily dissuaded from His plans.

The judges of Israel were often terrible people with no impulse control whatsoever. They were arrogant, violent, stubborn, and rebellious. If the Bible was propaganda instead of truth, it's doubtful their stories would have made it past the editors. But they are there, and they show how God used such sinful people to push the story forward. And just when you can no longer distinguish between God's people and the motley crowd around them, God finds an outsider to show us how it's really supposed to be done.

Her name was Ruth, and she was from Moab. She married a Jewish man who had moved there with his parents and brother because of a famine in their homeland. In a tragic turn of events, all the men in the family died, leaving three widows: Ruth; her Moabite sister-in-law, Orpah; and their Jewish mother-in-law, Naomi. The two Moabite women grieved their husbands, but they had never seen the special brand of grieving that is a Jewish widow. Naomi is recorded as saying, "I'm going to change my name to 'Bitter,' because God has been bitter to me. Now I'm going to be bitter to everyone else."

Orpah decides to stay put, but Ruth—for some inexplicable reason—decides to take Ms. Bitter back to Israel. I can only imagine what a fun trip that must have been.

In those days wealthy landowners were expected to leave portions of their fields unharvested so that widows and other needy people could pick the grain and have some food without having to beg. While Ruth was out there working in the sun, she caught the eye of a man named Boaz (who also happened to be a relative of Naomi's). Boaz, liking what he saw, asked his field hands to be a little extra sloppy so Ruth wouldn't have to work too hard. Naomi may have been bitter, but she wasn't blind. She saw what was happening and coached her daughter-in-law in just how to gain Boaz's attention.

One harvest night Boaz was all by himself. Having eaten a big meal, he fell asleep on the threshing room floor. Naomi knew this was Ruth's chance to make her intentions clear.

So what happened next? Well, . . . we're not really sure. A lot of ambiguous language is used, so scholars and commentaries run the spectrum on analysis. Some scholars like to assume the worst while others assume the best. While the details will remain private, whatever happened on the threshing floor that night is the first biblical account of a true relationship beginning with the woman's initiative. Boaz was attracted to Ruth, but clearly Ruth sought Boaz that night.

Neither Ruth nor Naomi was content to let life happen to them; they took initiative and solved their own problems. As in any good relationship (and all good stories), there are some bumps and detours, but Ruth and Boaz navigate them graciously; in the end it's amazing to see how quickly Ms. Bitter sweetens when a grandson arrives!

Meatloaf and Mashed Potatoes

Moab should never have even existed; the Moabites trace their lineage back to a crazy story we talked about earlier—the one about Lot and his daughters. If Lot had been a good guy and avoided incest, there would have been no Moabites. If the Israelites had done as God instructed, they would have all been chased out of the land a long time ago. But there they were, next-door neighbors, in fact. At least they had their own land and were willing to mostly keep to themselves.

And of all the books in the Bible, Ruth may be one of the least remarkable. By that I mean there are no miracles or feats of strength. Ruth doesn't seem to be particularly smart or talented; I don't know if anyone has ever thought to make a movie about this story. King David, Joseph, Esther, Samson . . . yes. But Ruth? This book is like the meatloaf and mashed potatoes of the Old Testament. It's the book of common sense, front-porch, homespun wisdom, the kind you get from your grandparents. It's not a thrill ride; Ruth and Naomi got up early, stayed up late, and did the kinds of things you have to do when you live on the edge of poverty. Boaz was a landowner, but he doesn't appear to be excessively wealthy; he seems more like a decent, middle-class guy—more substance than flash. Like when he followed the law to make provision for widows and orphans; granted, Boaz was a little extra generous once he saw Ruth, but he didn't take out a billboard announcing what he was doing. He just quietly went to his foreman and told him to be a little extra sloppy around the corners.

Once he found out that he was related distantly to Ruth, he put together a simple, practical plan to set things right. He went to the right people, in the right way, at the right time, and did the right thing. An ordinary story about ordinary people doing what it takes and doing what they should. All of the main characters are clever, simple, practical, hardworking folks—salt-of-the-earth types who help others and keep their word.

It's the kind of stuff we used to talk about but don't much anymore. We live in an age of innovation, which isn't inherently bad, but nothing will ever take the place of regular folks doing what it takes and doing what's right.

So what makes this a crazy story? Well, aside from the possible dalliance there on the threshing floor . . . and the scandalous history of the Moabites . . . not much. Except maybe this: God had said that His deepest desire was to bless everyone, not just people in Israel. So, when one of His people runs off and marries a Moabite woman, well, that's not going to stop God—He loves strays. He's always bringing them in at night, even though He knows that if you feed them once, you'll never get rid of them. He took in Rahab, and now this Moabite woman, Ruth. Orphans, widows, street urchins, mongrels—they all matter more to God than we think they should.

Just as rescued dogs have really good memories and rarely forget what it's like to be *this close* to death, rescued people have a similar response as recipients of the kindness of a benevolent master.

Another qualifier to include this story in the crazy category: the book of Judges leaves us with a decidedly pessimistic view of humanity. That's why we need the story of Ruth. She gets it right, even when we'd all give her a pass for getting it wrong. She's got the deck stacked against her. But she refuses to fold, choosing instead to play the hand she's been dealt with courage, integrity, and a dash of cunning. And what I love most is that there's no magic incantation to recite, no seven easy steps to total transformation in just fifteen minutes a day.

Generally speaking, most of us want to do the right thing, too. We want to get through the day and do a little good along the way. And when we pray, a lot of what we say goes something like this: "God, could you please make it easier for me to do the right thing?" Now there's nothing wrong with praying something like that. But what do you do when life gets tough? What do you do when obstacles in your path make doing the right thing difficult, and you're pretty sure God put them there? With a nod to Ruth, what are you supposed to do when you get stuck with a nagging, complaining, bitter, old mother-in-law who can't seem to remember that *your* husband died, too? Can you continue doing the right thing—even when you have to get up early, stay up late, and pick up the table scraps from somebody else just to put food on your own table? As crazy as this sounds, God thinks you can.

What makes Ruth's story so crazy is how normal it really is. You do the right thing by simply doing the right thing. Keep your promises. Share. If you see someone who needs help, lend a hand. When you see something you want, take initiative. This isn't rocket science; it's simple meat-and-potatoes stuff.

God's not really looking for the flashy. He doesn't need someone with superhuman strength like Samson to get His agenda done. Samson doesn't make it into the genealogy of Jesus; Ruth does. Ponder that one for a while.

God in a Box

IN 1 SAMUEL 4, the Israelites are fighting their archenemies, the Philistines. Today we use the word *Philistine* as a derogatory term for someone who is uncultured or uncouth. In reality the Philistines were advanced, particularly in the area of metal-working. They had mastered this new technology and kept it a secret from everyone else, including the Israelites. One major implication of this would be that when they fought, the Philistines used swords and spears while the Israelites used primitive weapons made of stone and wood. In a sense the Philistines had weapons of mass destruction. And they routed the Israelites badly.

In the aftermath the Israelites gathered to debrief, and of course the obvious question was raised: "Why? Why has this happened to us?" Then someone remembered their secret weapon: the ark of the covenant. As they prepared for their next encounter, they brought the ark with them.

The ark of the covenant was a box of acacia wood overlaid with gold. It contained the tablets of the Ten Commandments, a bowl of manna, and Aaron's old staff. On the top were two angels, and it was believed that God literally sat, enthroned, on those two angels. This was the manifest presence of God. So while Philistines had iron, the Israelites had the ark. The Israelites' rationale was, "OK, God, your honor is on the line now. If we lose this time, people won't just think about Israel as losers; they'll think Israel's God is a loser, too. You don't want the Philistines to think their god is greater than You, so You have to make us win now!" They know they can't lose . . . right?

Well, the story wouldn't classify as crazy without a twist. The Israelites lost. In fact, they lost *big*. The loss was so catastrophic that one man runs back to Shiloh with his torn clothes and dirty face to report it to Eli, the old priest. Eli is blind, so he can't see the man's sorry state, but he is told four pieces of information that go from bad to worse:

- It was so bad we had to run away.
- Before we could run away, we suffered heavy losses.
- Both of your sons were killed.
- They got the ark.

The news is so shocking that it kills Eli. His pregnant daughter-in-law hears this terrible news and goes into premature labor, with her death imminent. The midwife encourages her, telling her there is still hope because she is having a son. She tells the midwife to name the boy Ichabod, because the glory of God has departed from Israel. That's actually what the name means.

Ichabod is the negative form of *chabod*—the most important word in this story. Literally, *chabod* means "weighty or heavy"; figuratively, it means glory. Chabod was everything majestic; where chabod was present, there was dignity, meaning, purpose, and hope. But now all of that is gone. And the child's name would serve as a reminder.

The loss of the ark wasn't about losing a battle; nor is it about just losing some religious relic or object of historical interest. The ark is where God sat to reign over His people. With the ark gone, God was gone—which meant God either couldn't hear, didn't care, or wouldn't help.

So was the whole thing a lie? Abraham was just out there looking at the stars and talking to himself? No burning bush? These were all just fairy tales, and the ark was just a box? We've all lived horrible lives, and now we're destined to all die on the same day, so let's disillusion this son of mine from the day of his birth—he will grow up an orphan, and every time someone calls him by name, it will be a reminder that the glory is gone. That's the reality—Ichabod.

What God does next is crazy. God allows the Philistines to drag His ark from Ebenezer to Ashdod. He allows them to mock and taunt Him; we know this won't be the last time something like this happens. "He couldn't save His own people; He couldn't even save Himself," they must have shouted. He allows Himself to be captured. Unlike any other god of that world, YHWH took on the suffering, loss, pain, embarrassment, and humiliation of His people. He carries their shame on His back. What kind of God would do such a thing? And what was God going to do now?

The Philistines take the ark to the temple of their god, Dagon. They believed Dagon had triumphed over YHWH, so they place the ark at the feet of this statue of Dagon. Then they had a big feast, chanted all their favorite chants, told war stories, and then they all went home. That night something happened.

When the priests arrived the next morning, they discovered their god Dagon had fallen on his face before the ark of YHWH. Was it an accident? A coincidence? It almost looks like Dagon is bowing down to worship the God of Israel. This is not good for business when you're a priest of Dagon, so they dusted him off, propped him up, and held another all-day celebration. Once again it's nighttime, and with the lights out YHWH is left alone with Dagon. The next morning the priests make the same discovery, only this time Dagon's head and hands were severed and lain neatly across the threshold of the temple. The remains of Dagon were bowing down to YHWH.

The play-by-play details of what took place remain a mystery, but we know this took place over the course of three days. The first day is a dark day, and it looks like God is defeated: the glory is gone; heaven is silent; no one knows why. Some days are like that. The second day is the day of hidden combat, and it's shrouded in mystery. It's a day of ambiguity and anxiety. Some days are like that, too. But the third day? The third day is the Lord's day. On the third day we learn that our God does some of His best work at night. On the third day joy comes in the morning. On the third day, stones get rolled away, idols get disarmed, and people are filled with awe and wonder. One day will be like that. But that's not the end of the story.

The Philistines in the city of Ashdod are afflicted by a plague that is somewhat unseemly. Some say it was tumors; others say it was mice (the Hebrew words are similar), but some of the older translations are less afraid or ashamed to say it was hemorrhoids. Yes, He smote them with hemorrhoids. The Bible actually says they had hemorrhoids "in their secret parts" (1 Sam. 5:9 KJV)—which is the usual location for hemorrhoids, right?

Don't miss the irony: people who know how to work with iron need a soft place to sit. In God's presence we're all embarrassingly human, and no amount of iron swords or spears will help you when what you need most is a doughnut pillow.

The citizens of Ashdod called a town meeting and decided that maybe having the ark in their city wasn't all it was cracked up to be; maybe it was time to let someone else have a turn mocking the ark. So they send it to Gath. And it's not long before everyone in Gath is looking for a soft place to sit. The people of Gath decide to let the people of Ekron have a turn with the ark, but the people there won't even let it enter their gates—apparently word got around quickly, even back then. So all of the Philistine city leaders come together to figure out what to do, and they decide to just send it back to Israel. They call their priests together and ask them about the best way to do this. Their priests recommend a bribe to make sure this YHWH God is appeased. Their recommendation?

Five golden hemorrhoids and five golden mice. And just to make sure this isn't all a big coincidence, they come up with a pretty ingenious plan: They get a couple of milk cows who are still nursing and have never been yoked up before, and they hitch them to a cart. Then they take their calves away and pen them up. They put the ark on the cart with the golden objects and just let it go. They figure it would take a miracle for two mother cows to abandon their calves and know how to pull a cart like that all the way back to Israel.

The Bible says, "The cows went straight up the road to Beth-shemesh. They stayed on that one highway, lowing as they went; they never strayed to the right or to the left. The Philistine rulers were walking behind them to the territory of Beth-shemesh" (1 Sam. 6:12).

Gold Don't Make It Good

This is a crazy story with a lot of content and many, many deep theological truths we could tease out; but to be honest, all I can think about right now is what a golden hemorrhoid would look like. Move on, I must.

To begin with, the Israelites got offtrack in this story when their thoughts shifted from how glorious God is to how useful God might be. They stopped thinking about how God deserved honor and worship and started seeing Him as someone who could be manipulated into doing what they wanted. They thought they had God in a box; turns out, He doesn't stay there or in anyone else's neat, little box. You see, God refuses to be manipulated, and He cannot be controlled. He does the unexpected, and He goes where He wants. God is described in many ways; tame is not one of them.

In this occurrence He allows Himself to be taken captive and made fun of; He disarms false gods; He humbles the proud; and He uses milk cows to get His work done. In another occurrence the glory of God came to earth—not in a box but in a body. We beheld His chabod, one of His friends would write, but it didn't resemble our expectations. He had no money, no title, no power, no army, and in the end He was taken captive. His body—symbolically, a new ark of the covenant—was paraded through the streets to be mocked and taunted.

"You would save others? You can't even save yourself," they shouted. And Jesus took on the name *Ichabod* as he cried out, "My God, my God, why have You forsaken Me?" Then He died. His body—the manifest presence of God on earth—is put in another container that is sealed with a stone. And on the third day, we discover once again that we serve a God who does some of His best work at night when no one is around, a God who is perfectly capable of finding a way to get Himself free, a God who refuses to stay in the confinements we make for Him.

One last tidbit: the cows were lowing as they went, mooing as they brought God back to His people. What's up with that? I don't know. But I do know that one day Jesus had a parade with Him as He entered the city of Jerusalem. People were shouting and singing, and the religious leaders tried to get Jesus to make them stop. Jesus said, "If these people don't sing, the rocks will!" Maybe the cows knew that if they didn't moo, the stones would cry out. When God comes back to His people, someone or something has to make some noise!

2 SAMUEL 11

How Stuff Happens

IT WAS SPRING, the time of year when a king would go to war. Antsy from having spent the winter indoors, surely there was a border dispute somewhere in the kingdom that required his attention. Or a feud that needed settling. Something to get outside in the fresh air, ride a horse, raise the blood. But, for some reason, this year King David just didn't feel like going. He looked at his men, who were eager for his leadership, and said, "You guys go on without me."

He seemed bored. Listless. The text actually begins, "One evening David got up from his bed . . ." (2 Sam. 11:2). Evening? What was he doing in bed in the evening? As far as we can tell, David is about fifty years of age. He's not a feeble, old geezer, but he's not a young boy anymore either.

117

His eyes may have started to dim a little; his hairline possibly receding, or his waistline expanding. It's hard to age in public.

Once he was always so passionate, passionate about everything. But he doesn't feel that passion anymore about anything; he's restless and drifting. And there may be nothing as dangerous as a passionate man with nothing to be passionate about; he can easily become a danger to himself and to those around him.

There was a time when David would have talked to God about this. He used to talk to God about everything—good or bad. But now he's not even doing that. Maybe he doesn't know what to say. Maybe he's afraid God will give some terrible chore or horrible errand if he ever dared to tell Him he was bored. Whatever the reason, David keeps to himself, moping around the house, napping into the evening hours. And, as the text mentioned, one evening he gets up from his bed, wanders over to the window, and sees a beautiful woman next door, bathing on her roof. Something stirs.

We all see things we don't mean to see; it happens. Every person I know who has the Internet has eventually found something they can't "unsee," whether they were looking for it or not. You close the window, erase the history folder. Avert your eyes.

But David doesn't avert his eyes. He should. He knows that. But he doesn't. His eyes remain fixed. And then he sends someone to find out who she is. Her name is Bathsheba. But that's not all the information David receives. He is also told, "She's Eliam's daughter. Uriah's wife." David knew those men. Even if he hadn't known them, it should be enough for him to be reminded that this is someone's wife, someone's daughter. But David does not close the window or avert his eyes; he sends someone to go get her.

They have sex—perhaps because David just wants to feel something, anything. We don't even know if she was a willing participant. He is the king, after all. His orders are typically followed without question. The deed is done; she is sent away. And he thinks that is the end of that.

A few weeks later he receives a disturbing message: Bathsheba, Eliam's daughter, Uriah's wife, is pregnant. Uriah is in the military so he's away, fighting whatever battle David ought to have been out leading. Now David had a choice to make: he could come clean right now, apologize to Bathsheba, to her husband, to the nation, to his family, and to God. End it right here. But he does not. Instead, he sends for Uriah, has him brought home from the battlefront. He figures there's no need to panic; if he can get Uriah to have sex with his wife, maybe people can forget about math or think the baby came a little early. But Uriah, who isn't even Jewish by birth, proves to be a better Israelite than the king! David even gets Uriah drunk, thinking a drunken man couldn't resist the opportunity to sleep with his own wife; but Uriah has more self-control drunk than David had sober.

Ultimately, David sends Uriah back to the battlefield with a message for his commanding officer: David wants Uriah killed. Make it look honorable. Have him die in battle. But make sure he's dead.

After the deed is done, David takes in the grieving widow and marries her himself after an appropriate time of mourning has passed. We must keep up appearances, after all.

How the Mighty Fall

How in the world does something like that happen? It's one thing when someone has a pattern of rejecting God's ways. If this were a story about a godless, womanizing heathen, we wouldn't be surprised. That happens all the time.

You probably know people who lack integrity and moral values. Certainly, we've all heard of such people. If we heard they had done something like this, if we heard they were guilty of deception and all that, of using government personnel to assist them in their cover-up of a murder, we might be tempted to say, "Well, what did you expect?"

But this is David. King David. Writer of psalms. Killer of giants. The man after God's own heart. This is really out of character for him. He had loved God his whole life.

When David was a boy, he took care of sheep and knew that God was with him out there. He knew when wild animals came to steal his sheep, and he managed to drive them off. That wasn't his strength; it was God's, protecting him.

When he got a little older, he defeated Goliath. He did what no other man in Israel would do because he knew God was with him and would deliver him in battle. When he found himself in a cave faced with the opportunity to kill his rival, King Saul, David submitted to God's will and God's timing. He was so committed to obeying God that he wouldn't lift his hand to kill a corrupt king.

David was so passionate about God that the mere thought of God's presence returning to dwell among the people of Jerusalem inspired him to dance with all his might. In psalm after psalm David pours out his heart to God—asking God to search him, know him, and give him an undivided heart. He wrote about how much he loved God's law and how he meditated on it day and night. And yet . . . by the end of this story, David is guilty of lust, covetousness, deception, manipulation, adultery, and murder.

You don't just wake up one day and say, "I think I'll sleep with the neighbor's wife and then have him killed." That sort of thing doesn't just happen. But it sure seems like it did.

And messes like this one are usually considered career killers. David, the great and mighty king of Israel, coveted, stole another man's wife, committed adultery with her, lied about it, and had her husband murdered. That's five of the Ten Commandments right there. He's going to lose his job for sure now. He'll have to take several years off, probably go through some sort of intensive therapy, and find another career. Maybe he could teach somewhere in a few years. After all, how could he continue to lead God's people now? I've seen pastors publicly humiliated and forced to resign in disgrace for far less. And yet . . . that is not what happened. Not at all. Not by a long shot.

It's not that there were no consequences. There were, and they were terrible. The baby they conceived died, and his family comes unraveled to such an extent that eventually his favorite son murdered his oldest son. Then his favorite son stages a coup and humiliates David in a public way that you'll just have to read for yourself (2 Sam. 16:22). Eventually David's favorite general murders David's favorite son. Trust me: David was not off the hook. But God does not abandon David even though we may think He should and even though (given all the drama) it sure looks like He did. But four chapters before all this mayhem begins, God made David a promise: "I will make a name for you like that of the greatest in the land" (2 Sam. 7:9). Before you picked up this book, had you heard about King David? Promise kept.

In addition to fame, God also promised David a legacy: "'The LORD Himself will make a house for you. . . . Your house and kingdom will endure before Me forever, and your throne will be established forever'" (vv. 11, 16). Then four chapters later drama ensues, and it's all David's fault. Innocent people die because of him. It's a good thing we're not God because I know if I had been, I might have reconsidered my promise. But through all the chaos and bloodshed and disaster, God never withdrew His. And 990 years later, a man in the lineage of David named Joseph took his pregnant fiancée named Mary to the city of Bethlehem (also known as the City of David); and, while she was there, she gave birth to the great-great-great-great-great-great-great-great-great-great-great grandson of King David and Bathsheba. Because when God makes a promise, He keeps it, and not even the worst sin imaginable can force Him to go back on His word. You see, God's promises are based on His faithfulness—not ours.

2 KINGS 2

Don't Mess with Him

ELISHA WAS FROM a wealthy family; life was pretty good for him. If only he'd stayed put, he could have had a nice, comfortable life. You know the type: he had a nice job, picket fence, two-car garage. The whole bit. But sometimes God calls us to do things that don't make sense. In fact, the more you trust God with your career, the stranger your career path gets.

Elisha was out working in a field when Elijah came walking by. No words were spoken. Elisha knew. God was calling him to follow that strange, old man—to leave everything that was familiar and comfortable, just like God had called to Father Abraham all those years ago. He could not have known then that God would give him twice as much power as Elijah or be aware of the amazing and unbelievable things he would do and see. He could never have imagined the pain he would feel when pleading with his countrymen to return to God went unheeded. He only knew that this was the chance of a lifetime.

So in that moment Elisha chose to follow, to leave security and status behind, and to become part of a lonely line of prophets God used to call His people back to Himself. And that decision changed everything. After he watched his mentor taken into heaven by a fiery chariot, the miracles really started to happen.

First, he finds himself standing at the Jordan River. He and Elijah had been there earlier that day, and Elijah had taken off his coat and hit the water with it. The water had parted, and they had walked across on dry land. Now Elisha is standing there alone. He had Elijah's coat with him and figured he might as well try it out. Striking the water with Elijah's coat, the water parted and he walked through on dry land.

Next, some of the leaders of the city of Jericho met him and told him life in the city was great—except the water. The water was terrible, and things wouldn't grow because of it. He had them bring him a bowl of salt, which he throws into the water. From then on, the water was great and the land was productive.

Eventually Elisha would raise a young man from the dead, cause an axe handle to float on water, and take a small amount of bread and feed one hundred people. He would heal a Syrian general of leprosy and even foil a foreign army's attempt to invade Israel by asking God to strike them all blind.

But the really crazy story from what we know of Elisha comes when he leaves Jericho en route to Bethel. A gang of ruffians starts heckling him, making fun of the fact that he's going bald. They suggest that if he really was a great man of God, he would have been taken up into heaven with Elijah. Elisha calls a curse down from heaven on them, and then two bears come out of the woods and maul them. I'm not making that up. Two female bears mauled forty-two young men because they made fun of Elisha's male-pattern balding. That'll teach you, disrespectful kids!

Bears, Baldness, and Baaad-ness

OK, you probably don't often think of a man of God calling down curses on teenagers and being backed up by bears (unless, of course, you live with teenagers).

Three things immediately jump out at me. First, it doesn't seem like such a big deal, boys making fun of an old man. Second, the punishment does not seem to fit the crime—make fun of a prophet, get mauled for your trouble.

Third, the curse was from Elisha, but the actual punishment comes from God Himself, which makes God seem a little heavy-handed here. So, what are we supposed to learn about God here? He's supposed to be this wonderfully loving heavenly Father. He's not supposed to be ordering wild animals to tear people to bits.

To begin with, we should decide whether or not we're willing to give God the benefit of the doubt when we read something like this. See, when what you hear or experience falls short of your expectations, you can either fill that gap with trust or with suspicion. That's true in business, in your marriage, with your kids; and it's true with God, too. So how you read this story will depend, at least in part, on whether you fill that gap with trust or suspicion. If you choose—before you begin reading—always to give God the benefit of the doubt, then you can start to make sense of stories like these.

Also, we tend to think our culture is normal. That means all other cultures are abnormal or weird. When we assume our social mores are the right social mores, then we may find ourselves judging stories like this. But what if we're wrong about something? What if we allow stories like this to say something about our standards?

Most of the people reading this book are doing so from a safe place. We have police who serve and protect. We enjoy a level of unprecedented health and prosperity. Most of the people who have ever lived on planet Earth lived with violence and brutality as a mere fact of life. Justice was not normal; neither was safety. I'm not saying this to justify violence; I'm just saying we're especially repelled by anything that involves physical punishment when in fact we're the historical exception for that. So what if we retold the story, putting it in a slightly different context?

Let's say there was a king who lived a long, long time ago in a distant land—sometime in the sixteenth or seventeenth centuries, somewhere in Europe—and this king was called upon to settle a dispute between two clans in a nearby county, a border dispute of some kind. He goes out there, and something happens, like a heart attack or a stroke. And he dies.

One of the clans seizes this opportunity to attack the other side. They kill everyone and grab both plots of land. Word gets back to the castle and the young prince there. The prince now has to mourn the loss of his father and mentor, and he must come to grips with the fact that, regardless of how ill prepared he may feel, he is, in fact, the new king.

While he is processing all of this grief and anxiety, he looks out the window of the castle one morning to see a group of about forty or fifty young men from the clan just sort of milling about on the lawn. Soon they begin shouting at the castle, "You're not fit to be a king! Your father wasn't really fit to be a king, but he was better than you!"

Before long they really start to get personal with their taunts, making fun of his physical appearance. The new king is beginning to fear for his safety. How much longer until they set something on fire or begin throwing things? This could escalate quickly.

The young king musters up all his courage and shouts back at them. "You are all a disgrace to your family name and to this proud nation of ours! You should be ashamed at your lack of honor! Now go away! Return to your homes immediately!"

They laugh at his threats, but in the commotion some of the royal hunting dogs are alerted to the presence of trespassers. The dogs break free of their kennel and take off after the intruders, tearing them to shreds. One man lost a finger. Another lost a part of his ear.

The young men run away, back to their village. They are wounded, but they will survive. They may still dislike the king, but they know they must respect the office. And they'll think twice about going to the castle and stirring up trouble again.

We might hear that story and think those ruffians got what they deserved, talking to the king in such an uncivil manner. They're lucky the dogs didn't do worse. They're lucky it was dogs and not armed guards. They're lucky they weren't executed on the spot!

Now ratchet that up from a young prince to the spokesman for the God of the universe. What they had done was outrageous in their culture. Showing disrespect for God's prophet was the same as showing disrespect to the One who had sent him. That would be God, and that would be bad. They're lucky the bears only mauled them and didn't kill them. They're lucky God didn't rain fire down from the heavens. Seen from that perspective, God seems downright merciful just to rough them up a little and let them go.

For most of human history, the world has been a harsh place. Creation contains fire and wind, thorns and weeds that breed allergens. There are sharp and hard things in creation, and if you step out of line out there, you often get smacked upside the head. These young men weren't little kids. They should have known better; they should have known what they were doing was wrong; and they should have known that behavior like that might just get you a swift kick in the pants.

Disrespect for the holy and righteous God of the universe is a terrible and fearsome thing. I have a feeling that if we really understood the majesty and power of Almighty God, we would think twice before we excused these young men. And if we ourselves ever got to that point of understanding, we might stop thinking this story is harsh and needlessly brutal. We may even get to the point where we see in this story a kind of severe mercy shown to a city that is now served notice to keep them from a greater judgment that might come as a result of allowing God's man to be assaulted or killed.

If the Bible is going to connect with real life, it has to show us life as it actually is—not as we wish it would be. Life does not always give us storybook, happily-ever-after endings. In real life things don't always go the way you want. But through real life we learn what it means to be human. And that's what God really wants.

What Kind of God?

JOB WAS A good man who enjoyed a happy life with lots of children and lots of stuff. He loved God, and he loved doing the right thing. But then a weird thing happens: Job starts to lose everything. His house burns down. His kids die. He gets sick, and he ends up in a lot of pain. His wife begs him just to curse God and die. Of course, we like to attack her, but let's remember she's just lost all of her kids; I understand why she's a little angry at God.

Then Job's friends show up. At first this seems like a good thing. The best thing a friend can do in this situation is just sit there and keep his mouth shut. Just be present. And his friends do that for a few days. Then they open their mouths and wreck everything. They start accusing Job of somehow making God mad. Surely God wouldn't allow stuff like this to happen to a man who wasn't secretly looking at Internet porn or hadn't swindled someone somewhere out of something . . . right? God blesses good people and visits plagues upon people who misbehave. Job has been visited by plagues, so what is the logical conclusion?

They encourage Job to just 'fess up. God will forgive him, and they can all move on with their lives. But Job won't do it. He doesn't say he's never sinned; he just says that his spiritual life doesn't correspond to his change of circumstances. He lived a righteous life, and he was blessed. Then his blessings went away and were replaced by terrible disaster, but his spiritual life didn't change in such a way as to merit such a drastic change in his circumstances.

Now this isn't the whole story. There is another story going on in another place. God and Satan are having a conversation one day, and God essentially says, "Isn't that Job something? Do you see how much he loves Me? What a great guy!"

Satan's reply, my paraphrase: "Big deal. Job loves You like a kid loves the ice cream man. Stop giving him all this stuff and watch what he does. He'll abandon You because he's just using You."

God refuses to believe this about Job. God actually believes Job would serve Him even if all the gifts He's given Job went away. Job, being created in God's image, can choose love—even if love means sacrifice. So Satan pretty much says, "Challenge accepted," and the games begin. We should keep this preface in mind as the rest of the story plays out.

So Job's friends are making fancy, theologically astute-sounding speeches. Yet Job refuses to budge, eventually saying, "I wish I could sue God." And then the strangest thing happens: Job gets his wish. In fact, it's kind of funny. One of Job's friends is in the middle of telling Job why God doesn't have to show up when God actually shows up!

God never answers Job's questions. He could have explained about the whole conversation with Satan. But He doesn't; instead He just asks Job a few questions of His own, questions Job can't possibly answer:

Where were you when I established the earth?
Tell Me, if you have understanding.
Who fixed its dimensions? Certainly you know!
Who stretched a measuring line across it?
What supports its foundations?
Or who laid its cornerstone
while the morning stars sang together
and all the sons of God shouted for joy?
(Job 38:4–7)

Job realizes he is overmatched so he agrees to stop whining. And then God restores everything; in fact, the last part of Job's life was better than the first. The end.

Give and Take

What in the world is this story doing in the Bible? It's like a textbook primer on how to attack people who believe in a good God. If you're good, God might bless you . . . or He might burn your house down, kill your kids, curse you with a shrew of a wife, smite your skin with boils, and saddle you with the worst friends who will offer you terrible advice. Let's back up to how the whole story begins: "There was a man in the country of Uz named Job. He was a man of perfect integrity, who feared God and turned away from evil" (1:1). Uz was far away—east of Israel—and Job lived a long time ago. As best we can tell, he was a contemporary of Abraham. The story might as well begin: "A long, long time ago in a land far, far away." Anytime you hear a beginning like that, the author is trying to tell you that this story could be about anyone; this land of Uz could be anywhere, and the story could actually be our story. We all live in the land of Uz. And in Uz strange things happen. In Uz bad things happen, even to good people. In Uz bad things sometimes come without warning and without explanation. Uz is often a place of confusion and despair.

Next let's recognize that Job's not the main character—God is. God always is. That means what we think of as the plot isn't really the plot; it's just a subplot. And it means that the person we think is on trial isn't the person who's really on trial. We tend to think Job is the main character and is being wrongly treated by this supporting character named God. Consequently, we think God is the one rightfully on trial. But we should be careful here to make sure the God we find in Job is consistent with the God we find elsewhere in the Bible; too often, we make the God of Job into a bit of a jerk who shows up to flex His muscles so Job will just shut up. A lot of commentators seem to agree with Job's friends and end up missing the whole point.

So, why does God ask Job a bunch of questions he couldn't possibly answer? Is it just to show that He's smarter than Job? Is it because He's tired of Job's incessant whining? Is God warning Job: "If you don't stop all this crying, I'll really give you something to cry about?"

I don't think that fits with everything else we learn about God's character from the Bible. God doesn't seem interested in intimidating humans; after all, Jesus never used that tactic. It would be a little like me demanding that my daughters be impressed with how strong I am. They're kids! Only an immature and insecure person does stuff like that. "Look how strong Daddy is. Aren't you impressed? You'd better be!"

Instead, I think God is pointing out Job's limitations, especially his finite mind and limited perspective. And God knows that what Job really needs is not answers; Job needs a clearer picture of who God is. Job needs a clearer picture, not so he will shut up and take it like a man but so he will know what kind of God is in control of things. God's questions draw Job toward that clearer picture. Job's supposed to see that He's the kind of God who creates things in such a way that the morning stars sing together and angels shout for joy.

He asks:

Who cuts a channel for the flooding rain
or clears the way for lightning,
to bring rain on an uninhabited land,
on a desert with no human life,
to satisfy the parched wasteland
and cause the grass to sprout? (Job 38:25–27)

In Israel life depends on water. No one would waste water because it was such a valuable commodity. So why would God water a land where no one lives? Because God is good for no good reason. God is generous because He is. He does stuff like this without gaining anything in return; He gives because it's His nature. His entire speech in chapter 38 shows us a God who absolutely delights in creatures that are of no use to Him whatsoever. God gains nothing from doing any of this. But He does it anyway; it's who He is.

He created donkeys that will never be tamed, oxen that will never plow, birds that will never fly, hippos and crocodiles (behemoth and leviathan) that will never really be useful. This whole speech isn't about nature or animals; it's about the God who made nature and animals. These creatures are pretty much useless, but God created and cares for them. Why would God create a world and then fill it with useless things? It's what He does because it's who He is.

He doesn't need anything, so He doesn't take this utilitarian view of creation like we do. Maybe this is what God means when He says, "For My thoughts are not your thoughts, and your ways are not My ways" (Isa. 55:8). God's motives are not our motives. We're always concerned with how something is going to benefit us; God doesn't need or lack anything so He's not concerned with how anything is going to benefit Him. He's gratuitously good, irrationally loving, and ridiculously generous. In the end Job never finds out the why. Instead, he discovers something better: he finds out the kind of person God is. And that's enough for him.

SONG OF SOLOMON

Birds, Bees, Blossoms, and Wheat

THERE ARE SEVERAL poems in the Bible, but there is one in particular that is . . . well, for a lack of a better word, rather sexy. It's a dialogue between a man and his wife, and it gives us a glimpse of their private life.

It begins in the hill country, where a vineyard owner leases land to a family of sharecroppers: a mother, a couple of sons, and a couple of daughters. The oldest daughter is the ingénue in the poem. The boys didn't really care for this particular sister, and they made her work outside the home, which was unusual for the time. They were angry with her about something and made her take care of their vineyards and flocks. This made it impossible for her to tend her own garden and her own livestock. It also meant that she didn't have much time to take care of herself. Her hair was a mess. Her clothes were a mess. She was a mess.

One day she was out taking care of the sheep when she looks up to see a tall, dark, and handsome shepherd. She's never seen this guy before, and he's just staring at her. She's kind of embarrassed so she says, "I must look awful. The sun has not been kind to me." He tells her she's the most beautiful woman he's ever laid eyes on and that, if she doubts him, she should go look at the others. He compliments her skin, her face, and her neck. He babbles on for a good while.

Their chance encounter blossoms into a friendship that blooms into love. It's all terribly romantic, but then one day he leaves. He promises to return, and she promises to wait. She dreams of him at night. She looks for him everyday; she begins to wonder if he'll ever come back for her.

Then one day the king arrives in a great cloud of dust with his whole entourage—bodyguards, courtiers, a big royal chair. She pays no attention to him until he sends word that he'd like to see her. He comes to her tent, stopping at her door. She sees that the king is her shepherd, the boy from so long ago who had captured her heart. He tells her how beautiful she is, and she can tell that he hasn't changed a bit—probably because he still rambles on and on and on.

They marry, and their honeymoon is hot. Steamy. Not PG-13 stuff. More like NC-17 hot. The kind of stuff that gets banned from polite society. Rabbis did not want young men reading this stuff until they were thirty. And married. And alone with their wives.

So the honeymoon ends, and they go through a difficult time. For a while it looks like the fairy-tale wedding may not have a happily ever after. But, as the song ends, both the husband and the wife are confident and secure in their love. They sing of the lasting nature of true love, and they affirm their desire for one another, even after all this time.

Sex, Old Testament Style

I grew up going to church; in fact, my father is a preacher. I've probably heard more than two thousand sermons in my lifetime, but I can't remember anyone ever using Solomon's Song of Songs as their text. This is not a book that clearly teaches theology, nor does it contain any clear religious themes. It is not a book of history or prophecy. You will not find a collection of life principles here. It is not a collection of worshipful songs. It is not a book of lament. It does not end by saying, "And the moral of the story is . . ."

In its most literal reading, this is a book about the love between a man and a woman and their sexual expression of that love. And this has caused some angst on the part of biblical scholars. Of course, as you well know, when you don't know the answer to a Bible question, the answer you usually give is: Jesus? This is why so many Bible scholars say the book is about Jesus. It's not. You can find some parallels in there if you look hard enough, but on the surface this is a story about sex.

In a world so schizophrenic about sex, the church has mostly said, "When it comes to sex, we have one word, and that one word is *no*!" Evolutionary biologists and psychologists say the sex drive is all about procreation. The entertainment and advertising industries say the sex drive is all about recreation. People go to crazy places for advice, but the one place they won't go to with their questions about sex is the church. While the church claims to have the total truth—that is, truth that impacts every single area of life—our society knows better than to ask Christians about sex. They know we'll most likely say, "No! Stop! Don't do it! Turn back! Pretend it doesn't exist! It's yucky!" How in the world did we get that reputation? Don't they know we have a dirty poem in our book?

Before Christianity came on the scene, sex was considered something of a sacrament, a means of grace, a holy thing. In fact, Jewish people would often pray and recite psalms as they were consummating their marriage. Pagan religions, like the practices of Greeks and Romans, actually went so far as to include sexual intercourse in their liturgies. A temple prostitute, for example, would pray for a certain god or goddess to inhabit his or her body. Then you could have sex with that prostitute as a means of communing with that god or goddess. That's the religious atmosphere into which Christianity was introduced. So it didn't take long for Christians to push the pendulum too far in the opposite direction; in fact, Augustine suggested that sexual intercourse was how original sin was transmitted and believed that sex for any purpose other than procreation was sinful. Augustine was the guy who prayed, "Lord, make me chaste but not just yet."

Saint Jerome went even further and said that marital sex was only one step above fornication. According to Jerome, virginity was the ideal and should be maintained as strictly as possible. He is quoted as saying, "Anyone who is too passionate a lover with his own wife is himself an adulterer." Before long the church decided that since Jesus died on a Friday, there should be no sex on Fridays. Then someone remembered that Jesus was arrested on Thursday, so maybe we shouldn't have sex then, either. Of course, Saturday is the day He was dead, so having sex on Saturday seems wrong, too. We should take that day to think of Jesus' poor, grieving mother—who was a virgin when He was born! Oh, and what about Lent? Maybe we should give up sex for Lent. And Advent. And Pentecost. Eventually, once you took out all the days of fasting, feasting, and mandatory celibacy, you were left with only forty-four days of the year that were cleared for sex. And even then you were only doing it in order to get pregnant. Do not enjoy it!

Even one of the most amazing works of art was not safe from this school of thought. Michelangelo's Sistine Chapel, while a wonder to behold, features all-naked subjects. So one pope commissioned a painter named "Daniel the Trouserer" to paint clothes on them.

Around that time some pope decided all the priests should be celibate; then they banned the women from singing out loud because a woman singing out loud in public could inspire lustful thoughts in a man.

Eventually Victorian clergy advocated covering the legs of your furniture. What kind of man lusts after the legs of the furniture? Wait, don't answer that.

Here's what gets lost in all of our puritanical prudery: God actually created sex, and sex—when it's done right—is brilliant! It's amazing. It's astonishing. For starters, think of the anatomy of sex—the body parts used. The soft parts, the millions of nerve endings, the economy and irony of the design, the internal and the external, the combination of visual appeal and mechanical function.

Sex is not meant to be just functional; it's meant to be enjoyable. That's part of God's design. And the Song of Solomon is in the Bible as a testimony to this. Now I've heard people say that this book is not really about sex. I have been told that it is about Christ and His relationship to His bride, the church. I have to wonder if these same people have actually read the book. The people who read it initially knew that this is a celebration of sex and romance—no two ways about it. The man in the poem says this to the woman:

How beautiful are your sandaled feet, princess!
The curves of your thighs are like jewelry,
the handiwork of a master.
Your navel is a rounded bowl;
it never lacks mixed wine.
Your waist is a mound of wheat
surrounded by lilies.
Your breasts are like two fawns,
twins of a gazelle. (Song of Songs 7:1–3)

That does not sound anything like when the apostle Paul describes the relationship of Christ to the church. But wait—there's more! The guy in the poem is ready to get it on, so he kicks it up a notch with this: "Your stature is like a palm tree; your breasts are clusters of fruit. I said, 'I will climb the palm tree and take hold of its fruit.' May your breasts be like clusters of grapes, and the fragrance of your breath like apricots" (7:7–8). Even the worst literature student can figure out where he's going with this. So, how is a good, Bible-reading girl supposed to respond? Should she be ashamed? Should she slap his hands away?

The woman in the poem is not ashamed of what the good Lord gave her. She says, "I am a wall and my breasts like towers. So in his eyes I have become like one who finds peace" (8:10). She also says, "Let's go early to the vineyards; let's see if the vine has budded, if the blossom has opened, if the pomegranates are in bloom. There I will give you my love" (7:12).

Breasts like fawns. Flowers opening and blossoming. Mounds of wheat between a woman's thighs. That's straight-up sex talk. It's beautifully erotic. Solomon was a big fan of sex. And so is God. Regardless of how you read this book, a simple truth is unavoidable: there is dignity and a God-given beauty to true human love and the sexual expression that often accompanies it. To remove the physical expression of love is to remove a special part of God's gift to us—just as moving to the other extreme and removing love from the physical action removes God's blessing and the dignity of human beings.

EZEKIEL 1

The All-Seeing Eye

MOST PEOPLE LOOK forward to turning thirty because you're not a kid anymore but you're not over the hill. Usually you're established in your career and your family. Turning thirty is a pretty good thing for most of us.

For the Jewish prophet Ezekiel, however, his thirtieth birthday may have been the hardest day of his life. He had spent his entire life getting ready to serve in the temple, but, when he was twenty-five, war broke out and he—along with three thousand other upper-class Jews—was marched seven hundred miles away to the Chebar Canal.

Five years go by, and we can only imagine what he must have been thinking. *There must be some mistake! My life wasn't supposed to turn out like this! I've devoted my entire life to serving God, and this is what I get in return?*

Then something crazy happened. The heavens opened, and Ezekiel saw "a great cloud with fire flashing back and forth and brilliant light all around it. In the center of the fire, there was a gleam like amber" (Ezek. 1:4). It was probably like staring at lightning through fog. As he looked into this cloud, he could see four living creatures. Eventually, he figures out they're cherubim (10:1, 9–10), but at first he just describes them. Each of them had four faces (a lion, an ox, an eagle, and a man) and four wings:

> When I looked at the living creatures, there was one wheel on the ground beside each creature that had four faces. The appearance of the wheels and their craftsmanship was like the gleam of beryl, and all four had the same form. Their appearance and craftsmanship was like a wheel within a wheel. When they moved, they went in any of the four directions, without pivoting as they moved. Their rims were large and frightening. Each of their four rims were full of eyes all around. So when the living creatures moved, the wheels moved beside them, and when the creatures rose from the earth, the wheels also rose. (Ezek. 1:15–19)

There it is, right there in the Bible—proof of UFOs! No, I'm not talking the green alien kind. But it was an Unidentified Flying Object! Later some of the leaders of this exiled group of folks arrive at Ezekiel's house. While they're there, the Spirit of God shows him another vision. This time he sees the temple and a huge idol. Then he sees God's glory, just like he saw it before. It's like God is squaring off with this idol!

We know from Jeremiah that there were a lot of false prophets in Jerusalem at this time. They were saying Jerusalem could never fall because the temple was there, but God was showing Ezekiel that the temple itself would be destroyed and judgment would fall on Jerusalem. Ezekiel might have thought at that point that being so far from home isn't such a bad thing after all.

Some time later (chapter 10), Ezekiel has another vision of the platform and the creatures and the wheels and the throne of God, but now the platform starts moving from the center of the temple toward the door. YHWH is leaving the building! Where's He going? "The glory of the LORD rose up from within the city and stood on the mountain east of the city" (11:23).

Twenty years after his initial vision, Ezekiel is now fifty. He's still stuck seven hundred miles away from home, working with ten thousand other exiles. Now God gives him a vision of a massive temple. Its measurements aren't in feet or yards but in miles; it was gigantic. The description of it goes into great detail, including the dimensions of each wall and gate. Then Ezekiel "saw the glory of the God of Israel coming from the east. His voice sounded like the roar of mighty waters, and the earth shone with His glory" (43:2). That's where he had seen the glory head twenty years earlier. Finally, "the glory of the LORD entered the temple by way of the gate that faced east. Then the Spirit lifted me up and brought me to the inner court, and the glory of the LORD filled the temple" (43:4–5).

And that's the story of Ezekiel and his crazy visions.

Beam Me Up

Ezekiel's is such a crazy story it almost didn't make it in the Bible. Rabbis thought it was too strange, contradicting the books of Moses and revealing a scandalous image of God's throne. Yet there it is, tucked away between Lamentations and Daniel. So, what in the world do you suppose we learn about the character and nature of God from a man's visions?

It bears mentioning that there are actual books that have been written about the whole UFO theme of Ezekiel. I'm not saying they're good books; I'm just saying they're real (the books, not the UFOs).

Let's start by acknowledging that a lot of us have been where Ezekiel is. I don't mean physically, like the Chebar Canal; I mean we've been disappointed with life. We know what it's like to have our lives planned out, even to the extent of how we will serve God in some capacity; and then WHAM!—out of nowhere, life crashes into you, spinning you seven hundred miles from where you thought you'd be. And you remain there for decades, wondering why. How many times have our biggest hopes and dreams been sideswiped?

But God meets this displaced and disappointed guy, and in that encounter Ezekiel discovers something better than serving in the temple of the Lord: Ezekiel discovers the Lord of the temple.

In times of confusion, when circumstances are difficult to understand, when we find ourselves in situations we never imagined, our greatest need is to see God. When we allow Him to meet us where we are, we find we're right where He wants us to be. And then we can find the direction He wants us to take.

Now, as for that song we all know—the old spiritual, I have no clue how we got the idea that "the little wheel turned by faith, and the big wheel turned by the grace of God." There is no little or big wheel. It's a wheel intersected by another wheel, enabling the platform the four living creatures are carrying—upon which sits the throne of God—to travel in any direction (which would make parallel parking a snap!). Oh, and it can lift off the ground like a helicopter.

Here's what that means: God can go anywhere. Here's why that's important: Jewish people in Ezekiel's day thought God lived in a particular room in a particular building in a particular city. It's a good thing we don't believe stuff like that today, right? If we did, we might start to think of particular rooms in particular buildings as "sanctuaries" in "the Lord's house" and not let kids run or laugh or play in there. We might think we have to dress a certain way and act a certain way in those particular buildings.

In fact, we might begin to think God lives in particular cities that have a lot of those particular kinds of buildings—cities like Dallas, Nashville, or Atlanta—and that He does not live in other cities that do not have as many of those kinds of buildings—cities like New York, Hollywood, New Orleans, or Las Vegas. Yeah, it's a good thing we don't believe stuff like that today.

The folks down by the Chebar Canal would have been overjoyed to find out that God didn't forget or discard them—they're not missing out on having a relationship with God; they can still receive His protection and provision, even though they're not in Jerusalem. This would have been good news indeed.

But this was also bad news for others. The folks left behind in Jerusalem believed they were special—that God had preserved them because they were better than the others who had been shipped off to other parts of the world. They believed they had a special status because they lived in the right city and were able to visit the right building. They thought they could have hearts full of worms or decay as long as they lived in the right city and went to the right building to do the right rituals.

The wheels in Ezekiel's vision are covered with eyes. He sees everything wherever He goes. There's no place God can't go, and there's nothing God doesn't see.

As a child, our church would sing a hymn that creeped me out:

> All along the road to the soul's true abode,
> There's an Eye watching you.
> Every step that you take this great Eye is awake,
> There's an Eye watching you.
> Watching you, watching you,
> Everyday mind the course you pursue;
> Watching you, watching you,
> There's an all-seeing Eye watching you.[1]

Cue the scary music. We're being watched. The story goes that the songwriter (J. M. Henson) was at a revival meeting where he heard the revival leader tell a group of boys who had misbehaved the previous night, "We're expecting order here, and you had better be careful because there's an all-seeing eye watching you tonight." The revival leader meant the county sheriff, whom he had personally invited to the revival. Henson saw God as the ultimate sheriff and wrote the lyric above.

Usually, when we talk like this, we're trying to scare or intimidate folks into behaving. But when Ezekiel—turning thirty and living seven hundred miles from what he thought was his destiny—heard it, it meant something more.

Yes, God sees all of our bad behavior. But God also sees every hurt, every frustration. He sees all the rejection and confusion. He notices every time one of His kids does something for someone without getting anything in return. He sees your motives and your intentions, and He knows what you would do if you could. He sees the suffering of His children in prisons, orphanages, and hospitals. He sees people who continue to do the right thing, even when there is no visible reward. He sees everything—and for a lot of people, there's more comfort in that thought than there is warning.

Ezekiel was a desperate, confused, and discouraged man who must have wondered what God was doing in his life. But he saw the glory of God and realized that there's no place God can't go and there's nothing God doesn't see. And that was enough for Ezekiel. God is that all-seeing eye, but when you stop to remember that God is actually looking at us through a lens of love, it can actually be a catalyst for us to become the people God created us to be. Ezekiel may read like some odd science fiction movie, but it's more than that; it's better than that. It's a coming of age story. It's a love story.

Notes

1. John Melvin Henson, "Watching You." Public domain.

EZEKIEL 4

No Crazy like Prophetic Crazy

ONE OF THE more difficult things I had to do when writing this book was come up with the list of crazy stories. I don't mean it was difficult to find stories in the Bible that fit the definition of crazy; I mean it was difficult to limit myself to only thirty of these stories.

Take the prophets, for example. They play important roles in the Bible, and you always imagine them with such gravitas. But when you look closely enough at them, you find out some really disturbing things. I'd devote at least one, if not more, entire chapter to each one of them, but my editor tells me I'm on a deadline. So this chapter will be a kind of "prophet combo" of crazy. Here are a few tidbits:

- Isaiah walked around naked and barefoot for three years (Isa. 20:3).
- Jeremiah wore a yoke around his neck (Jer. 27:2) and hid his underwear under a rock (Jer. 13:4).
- John the Baptist lived in the wilderness and ate locusts and honey (Matt. 3:4).

Of all the crazy stuff prophets were told to do, however, I think Ezekiel may have gotten the worst of it. So let's revisit him, shall we?

First, we already know about his vision of a UFO that's covered in eyes and beings with either four heads or four faces flying all over the place—all on four monster-truck-sized tires. That's enough to make you wonder if this is the Bible or a B-movie from the 1950s.

Then God decides that the people aren't paying enough attention to Ezekiel's words and has the prophet become the world's first performance artist. He tells Ezekiel to draw a map of the city of Jerusalem about the size of a couple of shoe boxes. Then He has Ezekiel act out an attack against the city to show people how intense the battle will be: he built ramps, battering rams, and army camps. Way over the top, if you ask me.

So imagine a grown man in his thirties building a diorama of Jerusalem in the parking lot of the mall near your house. How would you feel if you saw him jumping around playing war, complete with army men and sounds of explosions, screaming, wailing, and any other self-made sound effects? Being the compassionate soul that you are, suppose you approached the man and asked him if he was OK. You ask if you could maybe call someone who could come help him? He looks at you with hollow eyes and explains, "I'm a prophet of God, and there's a war coming!" Given that response, most of us would think, *God's prophet is a crazy, homeless guy suffering from PTSD or something.* You might even call the cops.

But God didn't stop Ezekiel there. He then tells him to lie down on his left side and stay there for more than a year. Anyone who walks by gets a good earful about sin and judgment. Ezekiel stays like that for 390 days; then he turns over and lies down on his right side for forty more. While he's lying there, he has to eat, right? God tells him to make bread but also tells him he has to bake it over a fire using excrement as fuel. As with all other mentions of excrement in this book, I am not making that up—check me in Ezekiel 4:9–13. When Ezekiel objects to using his own, um, supply, God tells him it would be acceptable for him to use cow manure instead. Really? 'Cause that's better?

But wait—there's more! As if this is not enough, God kicks things up a notch by telling Ezekiel to shave his beard (did I mention that he had a beard—like a Duck Dynasty, I'm-winning-a-beard-growing-contest beard) and his head with a sword. He tells him to chop up some hair, put it in the middle of the map, and burn it.

This is beyond crazy. How is anyone supposed to take this guy seriously? If you were there, you'd probably avoid him and make fun of him. A bald-headed freak who eats manure-fired bread while lying on his side in front of his diorama of Jerusalem under siege, ranting and raving about sin, judgment, pain, and suffering is not going to talk me into repentance.

Art Imitates Life

The temptation for me now is to explain what this weird performance art piece means. That would be simple enough. Ezekiel is playing the role of God; God is the one who is really fighting against Jerusalem. The three acts represent the siege of Jerusalem (brought about by the long accumulation of sin in the nation); the suffering of the people in Jerusalem; those in exile (they have to eat a kind of manure-bread; that is, food will be so scarce that they will eat things that are unclean and will make them sick); and then finally, the destruction of the city and the terrible fate of its inhabitants (some will be killed immediately, some will die slowly, others will be scattered to the four corners of the earth).

But that's not what I want to talk about; instead, I want to talk about God. Specifically, I want to talk about why God would put His servants through such agony and turmoil. Why would God ask His prophets to act out such ridiculous things?

I know people in what I like to call "cool churches" who see this as a justification of the use of drama in their services since God had His prophets act things out. We can use acting, too, to communicate the message of God's desire to warn and save a lost and dying world—a message that many would rather not hear. And I get that. But we should also recognize that there are some significant differences between these prophetic "sign-acts" and contemporary drama. The prophets weren't just pretending to suffer; they were actually suffering. Their words and behaviors were delivered with divine authority. Their messages often took over the messenger in an all-encompassing, life-dominating sort of way. But really, since we're talking about the God of the people and not simply the people of God, we should ask ourselves: How does God communicate His desire to warn and save a lost and dying world?

If you think about it, you'll see that God Himself took on a prophetic sign-act. He didn't walk around naked or lie on his side for fourteen months. He did not act out a brief ten-minute sketch. He became flesh and lived among us for more than thirty years. He didn't wear a human costume; He became a human being. And in the ultimate sign-act He demonstrated exactly how God's justice and mercy meet. There, just as Jerusalem was once abandoned by God because of the people's sins, the Sinless One was abandoned by the Father—again because of the people's sins. There on the cross, naked and humiliated, He showed us His love and passion for sinners. In this sense the cross is the ultimate performance art—a show that is still often misinterpreted or completely ignored. It can show us the stark reality of sin's devastating consequences, as it refuses to comply with our delusions of adequacy, while demanding more than our best efforts and feeble attempts at holiness. It is not flattering to us. It does not allow us any hope of ever earning our way.

Now and forevermore, until He comes again, He has assigned to us a few sign-acts. Some call them ordinances; others call them sacraments. We are baptized into His death, visibly replaying the death, burial, and resurrection of our Lord. At Communion we receive the broken body in the form of bread and the shed blood in the form of wine. After this, we are each called to carry our own cross, recognizing that God's plan will probably include suffering as well as ecstasy, sorrow mixed with joy, pain mixed with peace.

Like the prophets of old, we are to allow this message to completely invade and inhabit every corner of our being. Some will consider our behavior odd, but we can take heart knowing that we are following in a long line of those who are more concerned with what God thinks of us than anything else.

The Madness of King Nebuchadnezzar

NEBUCHADNEZZAR WAS THE king of Babylon, and he didn't take orders from anyone. He was the most powerful man in the most powerful nation on earth. No one told him what to do—at least, no one who wanted to live very long. But God knew something Nebuchadnezzar didn't know: God had been using Nebuchadnezzar to prove a point. Now God is about to make that same point to the king himself.

He sends Nebuchadnezzar a dream that the king doesn't understand; he only knows it's important. It troubles him. He asks various people about the dream, but no one can help him. No one, that is, until Daniel.

Daniel wasn't from Babylon; he was from Jerusalem. Along with many of his friends and relatives, he'd been brought to Babylon against his will when Nebuchadnezzar invaded and conquered Jerusalem. Daniel knew that God had been using Nebuchadnezzar to teach God's people a lesson, and now Daniel knows that this dream will not be good news for the king. When God decides to teach someone a lesson, they get it. As the inventor of communication, He can be really clear when He wants to be.

This must have been frightening to Daniel; after all, Nebuchadnezzar did not have a good track record for being able to deal with bad news. The messenger often catches the shrapnel. Bad news for Nebuchadnezzar might equal bad news for Daniel. Understandably Daniel hesitates. In a nutshell, however, King Nebuchadnezzar says, "Lay it on me, brother." So Daniel does, and the outcome isn't pleasant. The king is not wise enough at this point to act on the truth, but at least he has it in his possession, and that is what eventually saves him.

God wants Nebuchadnezzar to acknowledge that he is just a human king and that there is One greater than he—One who is ultimately sovereign. God is the real King. God is the King of kings. He's the One who sets people up and can knock people down at His discretion.

Nebuchadnezzar isn't ready to admit that just yet, however. God basically says, "You're acting like a dumb animal who thinks he's really in charge of the household but doesn't realize there is a master who provides the food and the shelter. Acknowledge Me." Nebuchadnezzar refuses.

God warns that his stubborn refusals will result in humiliation—in fact, He might just turn him into the dumb animal he resembles. Had most of us been in Daniel's sandals, we would be thrilled at this point. We would want Nebuchadnezzar humiliated, removed from power, and made to live like a wild animal for a season—as long as we could bear witness to it.

Daniel, however, is a better man than that. Daniel has compassion; Daniel has mercy. Daniel warns the king and gives him an idea that may potentially spare him from the embarrassment to come. King Nebuchadnezzar has been told what is going to happen to him and what he might be able to do to avoid it. Then God waits.

A year later the king was walking on the roof of his palace. He said, "Is this not Babylon the Great that I have built by my vast power to be a royal residence and to display my majestic glory?" Cue the music: *bum-bum-bum*.

The words were still in his mouth, hanging in the air like a cartoon, when a voice from heaven said, "Fine. Have it your way." *Presto-chango*, the king is now a wild animal with feathers and claws. He ate grass; he was driven away from the palace and his people. We don't know how long he lived like that, but it was long enough. Eventually, the king, who had spent his entire life looking down on other people, realized he'd been brought so low that there was no one to look down upon. Finally, in his despair, he had to look up; and, when he did, he saw the One he had been avoiding for so long.

Presto-chango—the king was restored. His sanity, his majesty, his splendor, his status, everything. In fact, his greatness expanded. But now it was different; now he knew and acknowledged openly that everything he had came from Someone greater than he.

Deadliest of the Deadlies

God does not like pride. In fact, the Bible says, "Everyone with a proud heart is detestable to the LORD" (Prov. 16:5). That's not just a one-time statement against pride; the Bible says over and over again how much God does not like pride. In the New Testament, James says, "God resists the proud, but gives grace to the humble" (James 4:6). It's not just that God doesn't like proud people; He actively opposes them.

Obviously, this isn't talking about taking pride in your work or having a healthy self-esteem; this is about conceit, the quality of having an excessively high opinion of oneself, or one's importance—the sin of pride. That's what God detests.

This is strange to our ears. In our world pride seems annoying, but it doesn't seem like a fatal character flaw.

Browse through the self-help selections in a bookstore some-time and see how many books you can find that help you develop humility. While churches may discipline people for sexual misconduct or financial misdeeds, I've never seen an elder in the church dismissed for having a prideful spirit. And yet I'd venture to say that more problems are caused by pride.

Godliness and pride are mutually exclusive. I say all of this because everything that happened to King Nebuchadnezzar happened for one reason, which is given in the final sentence of the story: "He is able to humble those who walk in pride" (Dan. 4:37). Pride is one of the words songwriters love to use; it rhymes with lots of stuff, fits well into love songs—especially breakup songs. It's usually coupled with a particular word. Pride is never immature or unreasonable; pride is always "foolish pride."

And pride *is* foolish. It's also immature and unreason-able. And it's universal. C. S. Lewis says that pride is the one vice everyone struggles with; we hate it when we see it in others, but hardly anyone thinks they're guilty of it. It made the list centuries ago of the seven deadly sins. Most agreed that pride is probably the deadliest of the deadly sins, maybe even the one from which all the others spring.

I've heard some say that God doesn't want us to be proud because only He can be proud. I even read an article that discussed why God gets to be selfish and proud while we cannot. The main thrust of the argument went like this: God can do whatever He likes, and if you don't like it, He'll kill you. While I appreciate the focus on God and His sovereignty, I must say I find that argument philosophically and theologically shallow.

Plato wondered how it was decided that certain things were virtuous and other things were sinful. He asked if God (or the gods) just decided on a whim to prefer honesty over deceit, declaring, "Humans must be honest because we say so." Or is there something inherent within honesty that made God (or the gods) say, "We acknowledge honesty to be superior to deceit"? My answer is neither; honesty is superior to deceit because it more accurately reflects the character and nature of God. That is why we are told to be honest; honesty is godly. And it's the same with humility. God is not opposed to pride because it is something only He can possess; God is opposed to pride because pride is unlike Him.

For a brief time, God came to earth in the flesh—in the person of Jesus. One of the only times Jesus actually described Himself, He used words like *meek, humble, lowly*—words we typically do not associate with God, perhaps because we have crafted God in our own image and imagined how we would be if we had access to His power and resources.

This is why pride is so insidious: it gets in the way of my serving others; it resists the building of true community; it hinders the process of being transformed from within. This is the lesson God wanted Nebuchadnezzar to learn. It's not because He hated the king; in fact, it's because He loves the king and wants to be in a relationship with him. But the king's pride hinders that from happening.

So God loves Nebuchadnezzar enough that He is determined Nebuchadnezzar will learn this lesson about how destructive and harmful pride is, and he will learn it the easy way or the hard way. God's not in favor of the hard way; He wants you to choose the easy way. But He loves you enough to allow you to choose the hard way.

So He warned the king and then waited a full year before He did anything. He plants a seed in the king's heart and waits to see if it will take root and sprout a little. This demonstrates that God is amazingly patient; He waited to see if the king will take His warning seriously. He waited patiently, expectantly, hopefully. He gave sufficient time for the king to make the necessary changes. But after a year of waiting, God initiated the hard way. And Nebuchadnezzar got the point.

There is a happy ending to this story, though: "But at the end of those days, I, Nebuchadnezzar, looked up to heaven, and my sanity returned to me" (Dan. 4:34). This means more than just looking at the sky. Think about it this way: King Nebuchadnezzar had spent his entire life looking down on other people. Now he's been brought to such a low point that he can look down on no one. So in his despair he is forced to look up. And when he finally did, he saw the One he had been avoiding. He goes to God because there is nowhere else to go. And that's all God was waiting for.

All Nebuchadnezzar had to do was turn his gaze toward heaven to discover a God who loved him with an all-consuming love—a love that will discipline, if necessary. A love that waits for prodigal sons and daughters to come home. Yes, God could have forced the king to acknowledge Him; but God doesn't do that. God is so humble He'll let you bottom out if that's what it takes to get you to look up and see Him.

You Knew Better

KING BELSHAZZAR LIKED to drink. A lot. And, like so many others throughout history, while he was under the influence, he got a really bad idea. He gave orders to bring in the gold and silver goblets his grandfather had taken from the temple in Jerusalem. He wanted to drink his wine from them.

In the middle of the king's drunken party, a hand appears and writes three different words on the wall in a language the king could not understand. Then, just as mysteriously as it had appeared, the hand disappeared. The king was terrified; what he saw wasn't due to wacky wine, nor was it a hallucination. It was real. He called all of his wise men to decipher the message, but they cannot. Then the queen (his mother) remembered Daniel; he used to be good at this kind of thing. Maybe he could do it again. They send for him.

Now Daniel, on the other hand, was not given to many bad habits, unless you consider praying a bad habit. Just as the queen recalled, he had been a high-ranking official put in charge of an entire province—over all the other wise men. By now, however, Daniel was old and no longer in the king's service. King Belshazzar didn't even know who Daniel was.

When Daniel enters the room, he sees the writing on the wall. And he sees the new king. But if the gold and silver goblets from Jerusalem were still lying around, they probably caught his attention more than anything else. They would have reminded Daniel of what worship used to be like, many years ago before he was kidnapped. How long would it have been since Daniel had seen them? Did he recognize them as the ones from Jerusalem? If they really were still lying around, what was going through his mind and heart when it occurred to him how this king had used them? It would be insulting not only to Daniel but also to Daniel's God.

The king says to Daniel, "Do me a favor and tell me what that scribbling up there means. I'll make it worth your while." Daniel was secure in himself because of the God he served. He didn't have to prove anything to anyone. He'd been there and done that. But there was a time when Daniel hesitated before speaking truth to power; this was no longer the case. If this drunken, bratty boy of a king wants the truth, the truth is what he's going to get.

Daniel refuses his offers of reward and basically says: "Remember your father? How great and powerful he was? All of that power and greatness came from my God. And when your father got too big for his britches, my God turned him into an animal. Remember that? You know about all that, but you haven't humbled yourself. Instead, you set yourself up against my God by doing all this." Now none of this was what was written on the wall; this was just Daniel's preamble. From there, however, he moves on to explain to the king what the four words are and what they mean. The first two words were *mene (mene mene)*, which means "numbered." Kings get to choose a lot of things, but they never get to choose how long they're going to live. God already had Belshazzar's days numbered, and it's a lot lower number than anyone could have imagined. The third word was *tekel*, which means "you have been weighed in the balance and found wanting." God has seen everything the king has done. He heard every word and knows every thought. He has weighed it all on the scales of judgment, and the king has come up short. The fourth word was *peres*, which means, "your kingdom has already been broken up and taken away from you."

Numbered. Weighed. Broken. Four words to describe an arrogant king and his arrogant kingdom. Four words to describe us all. This was a sobering message, to be sure. And, in spite of Daniel's protests, the king hangs a necklace around his neck. Ironically, showing honor to one of God's servants is his last official act. He'll be dead before morning, and a new king will be in place—for now.

Stay Put or Move Forward

Everyone screws up. It could be leaving your cell phone in your pocket and walking into the pool or forgetting to pick your daughter up at school. It could be forgetting to set the timer on the oven and burning dinner, or it could be failing to save a document on your computer. We've all done it. When it happens, we all try not to curse and beat ourselves up for a bit. Then we move on. We know these failures are not fatal, so we don't allow them to eat up too much of our bandwidth.

But there are other ways in which we screw up, more damaging ways. We say the wrong thing, and those words cause permanent scars. We make terrible choices, and the consequences explode, harming our relationships and our own hearts in ways we never dreamed possible. But even these are not the worst kind of screwups.

It's one thing to screw up by accident. It's a whole other thing to do something you knew was wrong and have it blow up in your face—to have someone look at you and say,

"You knew better, and you did this anyway." And that is precisely what happens to Belshazzar in this story. He had seen his father Nebuchadnezzar struggle with pride; he also saw him humbled by the mighty hand of God. He knew better, but he did it anyway.

Now, his days are numbered. He has been weighed in the balance and found wanting, so his kingdom has been divided and will be given to someone else.

We all run the danger of thinking our lives are our own to do with as we see fit. God, however, has already determined how many days we will live. One day we'll all stand before our Maker and give an account for how we used our time. God knows when that day will be. It might be tomorrow; it might be another fifty years. We know it's going to happen, so it would behoove us to live in light of that inevitability. After all, we don't want to get there and have God say, "You knew this day was coming. Why didn't you live properly?"

God knows things we don't know. In this case He knew Belshazzar's reign was about to come to a screeching halt. An invading army was already beginning its approach, and the outcome would not benefit King Belshazzar. Just because you don't know something's happening, or it doesn't look like anything's happening, doesn't mean nothing's happening. We live in an age of instant information, and it's easy to think we know everything that's going on. But God has always done His best work in hidden and unseen ways—in secret places, behind large stones, underground.

According to two old historians named Herodotus and Xenophon, the Persian King Cyrus diverted the flow of the Euphrates River into a nearby swamp. This lowered the level of the river so his troops were able to march through the water and under the river gates. Many scholars think this was happening during Belshazzar's drunken party. Also, it was no secret that the Jews in captivity believed they'd only be there for seventy years; they could count as well as we can, and they knew the time was rapidly approaching for their exile to end. Belshazzar could count, too, and it may very well be that one of the reasons he used the golden goblets in his festivities was that he wanted to show that he didn't believe any of that nonsense. The Jews were here to stay as long as he was in power—which, as it turned out, wouldn't be very much longer at all.

God knows what He's doing, and He knows what time it is. He sees everything; and, though He's hardly ever in a hurry, He is always working, relentlessly moving His plan forward. Sometimes that plan moves forward because of you; other times it moves forward in spite of you. Make no mistake, though: it always moves forward. We can get on board or get run over. It's our choice.

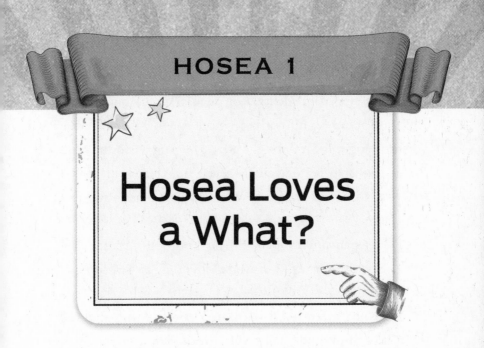

Hosea Loves a What?

FROM EVERYTHING WE know about him, Hosea seemed like a pretty good guy and a man who wanted to be faithful to God—more than a little bit unusual in his time. People during Hosea's lifetime didn't honor God; they used God when it was convenient. They never really stopped believing in the God of Abraham, Isaac, and Jacob; they just added other gods as they saw fit.

In other words, they were two-timing YHWH. So YHWH approaches Hosea with a strange command. He tells Hosea to marry "a promiscuous wife" named Gomer.

Maybe she was beautiful; maybe they knew each other; or maybe they were in love. We don't really know. We do know that God tells Hosea how the whole thing would turn out: she would be unfaithful. She would intentionally enter into a lifestyle of infidelity, not once or twice but habitually. Talk about cognitive dissonance. Imagine being Hosea. You're trying to be an upright person, trying to do the right thing, trying to honor your Maker. And then your Maker tells you to marry someone who will break her vows and your heart.

There aren't many people who know in advance that when they say "for better or worse" it's going to be primarily the latter.

They had a few good years after the wedding and had three beautiful children. But God tells Hosea to give each child a terrible name. Jezreel was a place where a massacre had occurred. Lo-Ruhamah means "not loved." Lo-Ammi means "not my people." And then Gomer began to stray. It was probably subtle at first, but before long everyone in town knew what was going on. Hosea was humiliated. Eventually, she left altogether and ended up being sold into slavery.

Now divorce would have been a legitimate option for him, but Hosea wouldn't pursue that. First of all, God had commanded him to marry her; he hadn't said anything about divorce. More than that, though, it seemed as if Hosea's heart had grown attached to this wayward woman. As angry and hurt as he must have been, his love for his wife overpowered his desire for justice. Rather than paying

Gomer back for the pain and suffering she had inflicted upon him, Hosea took a different approach. He pursued her until he found her, and then he bought her out of the trouble she'd gotten herself into. He literally purchased his wife out of bondage and brought her back home. Of course, this raised a question: Would she remain faithful this time? Is it possible that love and acceptance can accomplish what judgment and condemnation never would? Would this wandering woman allow herself to find the unfailing love she really desired in the arms of her one true husband?

The Biblical Side of the World's Oldest Profession

What's up with the Bible and prostitutes? The Bible is full of them. Rahab helped save the Israelite spies in Jericho; Jesus spent time with "women of ill repute" while He was here on earth—even telling people that prostitutes are entering the kingdom of God (Matt. 21:28–32). They are present throughout the story of Scripture; if it's not "the world's oldest profession," it's bound to be close. God includes them in His story, using them to further His mission or to illustrate a point.

Some of the most famous women in history have been tainted by sexual sin—just look at the genealogy. Four women are mentioned (which is odd in and of itself), and they're all sketchy:

- Tamar—who pretended to be a prostitute to get her father-in-law to impregnate her
- Rahab—whose name is almost always followed by the phrase "the harlot"
- Ruth—who threw a forward pass at Boaz on the threshing-room floor
- Bathsheba—who had an affair with King David

Seems like there might be a theme going on here. God loves wayward women with an irrational sort of love—a love that defies common sense, a ridiculous love, a love that causes Him to do stuff we would never dream of doing. And this is a very good thing because I, too, am a prostitute. And more than likely so are you. God's people have always been this way. We sin, and we hurt the One who loves us most. Sometimes we do this in big ways; sometimes we do this in small ways that are hidden and quiet. The fact remains, we've all broken our vows with God in one way or another.

Throughout most of Hosea's life—and throughout most of the Old Testament—God's people two-timed Him, three-timed Him, four-timed. . . . They had this covenant relationship with Him, but then they also kept these other gods on the side. Hosea's marriage was a mirror reflecting God's relationship with His people.

You see, God said, "I do" with full knowledge that we would be unfaithful to Him. God knew we would get ourselves into trouble we could not get ourselves out of. He knew our deliverance would be up to Him, and He knew precisely what that would involve. And He did it anyway.

God could have divorced Himself from me a long time ago. I've adulterated my promises to Him, breaking more vows to Him than I can remember. According to Old Testament law, I deserve the death penalty many times over.

But God loves me with a crazy sort of love. In Hosea's story God seems to waver for a moment (Hosea 11:5–7), but He can't seem to live with that course of action so He relents (11:8). God cannot allow judgment to be the last word; His prevailing love refuses to give up.

So the question we must answer is this: When faced with our own infidelity, will we return to our first love or continue in our betrayal of it? Will we turn from our waywardness and run to the arms of the One who purchased us out of slavery and eagerly awaits our return? Let me put it in biblical terms—will we *repent*?

We all have weird baggage associated with that word. It's been misused. It's the subject of manipulation and coercion. But *repent* simply means to recognize you're headed in the wrong direction and turn around to go the right way again. Once we acknowledge our adulterous ways, we must repent and make a commitment to return to the path God has chosen for us. That path includes loving others the way God has loved us. Hosea teaches us that godly love isn't impulsive; it's a decision. It is a firm commitment to act in the best interests of the beloved, regardless of the cost. Hosea made a decision to love Gomer, knowing the steep price he would have to pay.

Hosea loved Gomer. That's why he married her, even though he knew she would be unfaithful. That's why he stayed married to her, even though he knew he would have been completely justified pursuing divorce. That's why, when she was at her lowest point, he paid her ransom and brought her home. He loved her.

The Bible assures us that God loves the world in the same way. That doesn't mean He feels warm fuzzies toward us; God knows us too well to feel like that for very long. He sees our sin, and sin is always repulsive to Him. Still, He has chosen to act in our best interests regardless of personal cost, even to the point of sacrificing His Son to redeem us.

God's love for us has been demonstrated not only through the sacrificial death of His Son but in this: "God's love has been poured out in our hearts through the Holy Spirit who was given to us" (Rom. 5:5). The Holy Spirit pours God's love into our hearts so that we can personally experience it in our lives today. Moreover, once we have internalized this love, then we can choose to act—painful as it may be—by the power of the Holy Spirit, in the best interests of others. Just like Hosea did. Just like God does.

Yes, God has a thing for prostitutes. But let's be real about what that really means. It turns out that the prostitute is not some woman with a weird name who lived thousands of years ago but, in fact, is the face that greets you every morning in the mirror.

Insights from the Inside (of a Fish)

JONAH WAS HANGING out at home, minding his own business, when God showed up and told him to travel five hundred miles to the city of Nineveh. He instructed Jonah to tell them that if they don't straighten up and fly right, He was paying them a visit. So Jonah immediately got up and ran the other way.

Not quite the heroic behavior we normally expect from a prophet in the Bible, but that's what he did. He went to the docks and grabbed a seat on the first ship out of town, which happened to be heading two thousand miles in the exact opposite direction from Nineveh. He paid his fare, went below deck, and fell asleep, thinking he had managed to escape from God; but God's not that easy to escape.

A huge storm woke Jonah up—literally and figuratively—and, after confessing to his shipmates that he was the cause of the bad weather, he asked to be thrown overboard. Maybe he figured drowning in the sea would be a good excuse for not completing his assignment because Jonah really did not want to go to Nineveh. The people there were godless heathens who did not take kindly to strangers showing up telling them what to do. But God wasn't ready to let Jonah off the hook that easily; He had a message for the Ninevites. And as odd as it must have sounded to Jonah, God actually cared about the crazy pagan people up there. He didn't want them to keep going the way they were going; He wanted someone to go warn them. Maybe they'd turn to Him, and He'd finally have a relationship with them.

Rather than allowing Jonah to retire to Davey Jones's Locker, God sent a big fish to swallow Jonah, and it swallowed him whole . . . and alive. So Jonah had some time to think about what he had done. There, in the belly of that fish, Jonah came to his senses and told God he was sorry. A few days later the fish started to wonder if maybe he'd eaten some bad human, and Jonah became the first person to find out whether or not a fish's eyes water when it throws up.

Jonah went to Nineveh and delivered his message, all the while hoping the people would ignore his warning so God would destroy the whole place. He'd probably heard about what God did to Sodom and Gomorrah. That was the sort of action he wanted to witness.

His message delivered, he found a nice spot on a hill at the edge of town from which he could watch the divinely inspired fireworks. But the fireworks never came. Jonah's message was more powerful than he reckoned. Or maybe it was the power of God coming through his message. The people of Nineveh actually took him seriously, turned things around, and cried out to God. And God heard them.

Jonah sat up there on that hill and just got madder, and madder, and even madder. First he was mad at the Ninevites. Then he was mad at God. Then he was mad because it was crazy hot up there on that hill! And God, because He's God and He is merciful, had a plant grow quickly and provide some shade for Jonah. That seemed to calm Jonah down a little. Then God, because He has a highly developed sense of humor, had a worm eat the plant and take away Jonah's shade. Now Jonah was really hot, and he let God have it! I imagine the conversation went a little something like this:

"Oh, why don't You just kill me, then?!" Jonah said.

"What? Are you this angry about the plant, Jonah?" God replied.

"Yes, I am! Besides, I knew You were going to let them off the hook! I knew You wouldn't really kill them all! You'll kill this plant, but not those people," Jonah screamed at the sky.

"Is that what you wanted, Jonah? You want Me to kill them all? I wanted them to change. There are more than 120,000 people down there who don't know their right hand from their left when it comes to morals and values. You're sitting up here at a safe distance, and I think you care more about the plant than you care about those people."

"Harumph!" said Jonah. And that was the end of that.

Flight Risk

Sometimes we're so familiar with a story that it doesn't sound crazy to us until we start to tell someone who has never heard the story before. Try telling someone that a grown man was swallowed whole by a giant fish, then survived being thrown up by that fish, and see what they say. They'll tell you: that is a crazy story.

Growing up in church, this story was about two things. First, it was about proving to people that it actually could happen. If a person didn't believe this could literally happen, they might not believe anything in the Bible literally happened. Oh, and it had to be a fish—not a whale. A whale is a mammal, and the Bible clearly says it was a fish. This is another part that sounds crazy when you start to tell someone else.

Second, the moral of the story for us was clear: If you run from God, He'll send a storm to shipwreck your life, and then you'll end up being swallowed by a fish so you can think about what you've done until you're good and sorry. That can't be right, can it?

Let's think this through. In the story of Jonah, we see a man who hears a call from God. He chooses to run from the God of the universe by getting on a boat for several days. In the middle of the sea, Jonah would be completely helpless. OK, so Jonah's not the smartest prophet in the Old Testament.

Still, when he hits rock bottom, he cries out to God. God then does something amazing. God hears and He answers. No "I told you so" lectures. No "how sorry are you?" questions. God hears and He answers. Why? Because God loves people—flight risks, sailors, even Ninevite heathens. He warns heathens. He spares sailors. He disciplines flight risks. And He does it all because of His great love.

That last one is a major theme in the Bible: God disciplines people because He loves them. His discipline isn't sent to pay us back but to bring us back. The text actually says something that sounds a little crazy until we think through this particular lens: "Now the LORD had appointed a huge fish to swallow Jonah, and Jonah was in the fish three days and three nights" (Jon. 1:17).

Appointed? Some translations even say "provided." I don't usually associate the Lord's provision or divine appointments with something like this; I think of God providing food in the midst of famine or money in the midst of poverty. God provided a child for a barren woman. God provided manna in the wilderness. Being swallowed by a huge fish is hardly my idea of provision.

Then again, if I think of God's discipline as a sign of His love, it makes a little more sense. God doesn't want Jonah to die; if He doesn't intervene, Jonah is going to drown out there. God provides rescue in the form of a fish—that kinda makes sense to me. By far, however, the bigger message of Jonah's crazy story has to be what we learn about God from His interaction with the Ninevites.

God doesn't want to destroy the city of Nineveh, so He sends a warning through Jonah; Jonah doesn't value those people as much as God does, however. It becomes increasingly clear that Jonah doesn't want to warn them because he thinks they might actually repent and be spared. Jonah would rather see them die than have them united with the God who created and loves them. In the end we find Jonah resigned to doing the will of God but doing it through gritted teeth. No lesson learned.

Here's a guy who got a second chance, yet doesn't want the Ninevites even to have a first chance. They're outsiders so he shouldn't have to care about them. He knows he's supposed to love his neighbors as he loves himself; he just figures the Ninevites aren't his neighbors. Jonah's not the first person to do this, and he's not the last, either. It still happens all the time. It's easier to put a group of people into the "not-my-neighbor" camp than it is to go and figure out how to love them.

God loves everyone, even those who fall into categories we don't like to think about. He sent his Son to live and die and come back from the dead on their behalf, and He does not want any of them to spend eternity separated from Him. He loves them as much as He loves you. That may be hard to hear, but it's true. And He calls those of us who have entered into a personal relationship with Him to turn and show the same kind of love to them that He has shown to us.

Jesus, Legion, and the Pigs

ONE DAY JESUS looked at His friends and said, "Let's go over to the other side of the sea." It had been a long day, and Jesus had been teaching a large crowd—so large, in fact, that He had to get into a boat and push back from the shore a little just to be heard by everyone. It was evening so it was probably starting to get hard to see Him anyway.

So they shoved off and started across the lake; Jesus falls asleep. During His nap a pretty serious storm blows up. The wind gusts, and the waves batter the boat. The disciples are afraid they're going to die. They wake Jesus up, shouting, "Don't you care if we die?" Jesus gets up, hair probably askew, pillow marks on his face, and says, "Be quiet!" It's important to note that He said that to the sea—not to His disciples. In an instant everything goes calm. Jesus looks at His friends and says, "Trust Me; you don't have to be afraid."

And they look at one another wondering, *Who is this Guy?* That's also the central question Mark's Gospel asks: Who is this Guy who teaches like no one we've ever heard before? Who is this Guy who heals the sick and raises the dead? Who is this Guy who commands the wind and the waves? That question is about to be answered in a really crazy story.

They land on the eastern side of the lake—a place where Gentiles live. It's late, probably sometime between 9:00 p.m. and midnight. As soon as they get out of the boat, a zombie comes running at them. At least, that's probably what he looked like. It was actually a guy who had demons living in him. He lived in a graveyard. I don't want to think about what he ate. He's a cutter. The townspeople had tried to restrain him with chains, but he had broken them apart, so he's got to be quite strong. Sounds like a zombie to me. Oh, and he's naked—a naked zombie.

Well, no doubt the disciples were officially freaked out now, having just survived the terrible storm in which they thought they were going to die. They've arrived in a strange place wet, scared, and tired. And now this. A weirdo runs up to their Leader, shouting and looking like death warmed over. And he yells, "What do You have to do with me, Jesus,

Son of the Most High God? I beg You before God, don't torment me!" (Mark 5:7).

Let's get this straight: It was a dark and stormy night when an undead naked man came running at them from among the tombstones, dragging chains behind him. This is exceedingly spooky. And just ahead, on top of a hill, was a pig farm. Not the most pleasant smell in the damp, night air. It smells like death and swine, and all that comes with them. Everything about this scene screams, "Get the heck out of here!"

But Jesus wanted to come here. He was neither afraid nor uncomfortable; He just spoke to the zombie dude, saying, "Be quiet. It's time to go." The demons inside the guy have one last request. "Don't send us away. Let us go into that herd of pigs on that hillside over there." Jesus says OK. The demons go into the herd of pigs, and two thousand pigs run down the hill and drown themselves in the lake. Imagine the awful noise, panic, and squealing. And then . . . silence. Calm. If only for just a moment.

Meanwhile the disciples now have two things to process: the storm on the sea and the dude with the demons. Back at the pig farm, the owners of the pigs do not appreciate this. As far as they are concerned, Jesus has just killed their pigs. Now they're asking the question, "Who is this Guy?" Whoever He is, they want nothing to do with Him, so they beg Him to leave before He costs them any more.

So Jesus gets back in the boat. The now-healed former zombie guy begs to come with Jesus, but Jesus denies his request. He wants the guy to stay behind and tell people what happened to him. Jesus and the disciples get in the boat and leave.

Fright Night

I have so many questions about this story. First of all, why are there so many demon-possessed people running around Israel in the first century? Second, why does Jesus talk to demons? How freaked out were the disciples? And what is up with the demons wanting to go into the pigs? And why in the world does Jesus let them go? That's just the list off the top of my head. If I think about it anymore, my brain may just give me the color wheel, and I'll have to force-quit this story.

We're not used to thinking of Jesus as scary. That doesn't fit the description we normally get. I think of Him as kind and compassionate, humble and unassuming, funny, warm, smart, and many other adjectives; but I do not often think of Him as scary. And yet these people who are closest to Him are unavoidably afraid of Him—terrified really.

Jesus has power; He did and still does things only God can do. When you come face-to-face with that kind of power, it's not only awe inspiring; it's frightening.

Some people think demon possession still happens today. There are no shortage of churches and ministries devoted to deliverance (or healing, cleansing, etc.). They'll pray over you, anoint you with oil, and call out demons by name.

Regardless of your beliefs on demon possession now, then, and throughout space-time-history, here's what I do know: demons dehumanize. When people stop acting human, it's because there's something demonic or satanic at work. The man they encounter in the story is hyperactive, naked, cut off from community, self-destructive, and miserable. That's the opposite of what he was created to be. He was created in the image of God to enjoy life with dignity. He was created for relationships. He was created to love life, to love God completely, himself correctly, and others compassionately.

He's not human when Jesus meets him. Jesus confronts him, and the word that's used here is the same word that's often used when two hostile powers meet on a battlefield. Clearly this was some sort of showdown, which explains why Jesus has this conversation with those demons. It doesn't explain why Jesus grants the demonic request regarding the pigs, however. Jesus commanded the wind and the waves; surely He commands the demons as well. He can defeat them, even when He is outnumbered.

Some suggest that because Jesus was Jewish He hated pigs. It's true that the Old Testament said Jews could not eat pigs, but it didn't say they had to hate pigs. This isn't about Jesus being Jewish; it has more to do with Jesus wanting people to see what demons do. Demons are destructive by nature; if they can't destroy a person, they'll destroy a pig. Changing the object doesn't change the objective: steal, kill, and destroy. Also, there can be little question that the demons are gone from the man now, right? He knows the demons aren't in him anymore. The people around there know that the demons aren't in him anymore. Oh, and they all know the demons were really there to begin with. This guy wasn't faking. And all of that is known because Jesus allows the demons to go into the pigs. Now no one is really thinking about the demons, or the pigs, or even the man. They're thinking about Jesus—the One who had power over them all. Who is this Guy?

In the middle of all the chaos and confusion, there's one man sitting calmly, probably for the first time in years: Zombie Dude. Because he was delivered. Healed. Cleansed. Restored. And he knows the truth. He knows it in a way no one else there does. He knows who Jesus is. The words may have come from a demon, but they came out of his mouth. Jesus is the Son of the Most High God.

If you really want to know who this Jesus guy is, don't look at the storm. Don't look at the graveyard, the demons, or the herd of pigs. Look at the man sitting there with a clear head. Where is everything that once threatened to undo him? It is broken and gone in the face of Jesus' power.

Jesus entered an unclean land, encountered an unclean man living in unclean conditions and possessed by unclean spirits. Jesus sent the unclean spirits into a herd of unclean animals. The Son of God is willing to travel land and sea to restore human dignity. And in the wake of all of that sits one man who will never forget what has happened to him—one man who will tell everyone he meets from now on about this Jesus Guy who is the Son of the Most High God. Sure sounds like good news and gospel to me.

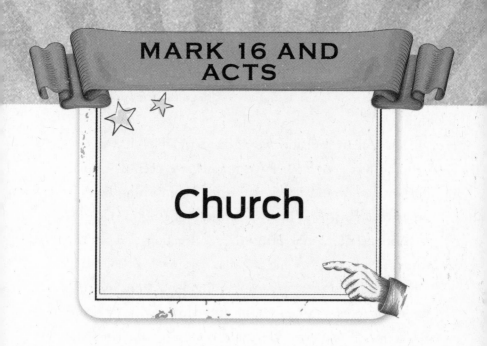

Church

FOR THREE YEARS these guys watched the greatest story of all time unfold before their eyes and were actively involved in it. It was amazing, the adventure of a lifetime. They watched as He taught, lived, healed. He was confusing and challenging, yet always loving—even when He admonished them or sent them out to do impossible things. He was the smartest, most amazing person they had ever known; they didn't even know a life like His was possible until they saw it for themselves, up close and personal.

And then the unthinkable happened: He died. They saw Him dragged out of a garden and put on trial on some trumped-up charges. They saw Him flogged—or at least they heard the awful details about it—then they saw Him suffer and die. They saw His corpse—there was no mistaking His fate. What in the world could they have been thinking?

Most of us probably would have thought that was the end and just gone home. We would have been devastated, but we also would have returned to our fishing boats or other vocations. And then the greatest ending to the greatest story ever told took place: the resurrection. A dead Man came back to life! No one saw that coming.

He had told them He was coming back from the dead, but no one was waiting for Him at the tomb with "Welcome Back, Jesus!" banners. He came back with no fanfare in the quiet hours of a spring Sunday morning. No one was around. A few guards nodding off at their post, suddenly bowled over by whatever it was that rolled that stone away. None of the people who said they believed in Him so much that they would follow Him through the gates of hell were even there. He said He was coming back, but they locked themselves indoors out of fear. He had to go looking for them.

When He found them, they didn't really believe it was their Lord until He showed them His scars. Now they must have been wondering: *What is He going to next? How do you follow a resurrection?*

They could think of only one thing that would top that, so they asked Him, "Are You finally going to kick the

Romans out, seize the throne, and make Israel the envy of all the other nations?" After reviewing some instructions, Jesus basically said in response to their question, "Tag! You're it!" Then He left. Disappeared. Vanished. Ascended into heaven like Neo at the end of *The Matrix* (only without the industrial music).

Um, beg pardon? This was not what they were expecting. They probably figured they'd just continue to tag along with Jesus, watching Him do His thing and getting to play a supporting role now and again. Instead Jesus leaves. I wonder how long they stood there looking up at the sky, thinking He'd be back any minute. Thinking, *Maybe Jesus is just punking us? There's no way He'd leave us in charge. Seriously, we have no idea what we're doing.* Eventually, a couple of angels come along and shoo them away. "You heard what He said. Go on. Get out there!"

So that's what they did. They got out there, and they messed some things up, they got some things right, and they turned the world on its ear. They didn't know what else to do, so they did what they remembered seeing Jesus do. They prayed. They talked about God and the kingdom and salvation. They forgave. They endured. They loved. They told the truth. They modeled selflessness and service. Jesus had said they would be His witnesses, so they did what witnesses do: they told people what they had seen, heard, and experienced.

They had no strategic plan. No resources. No buildings. No staff. But they found out that if you can talk to people about Jesus—in open, honest language they could understand—things start happening. They found out that if you do the kinds of things Jesus did, you get similar results. It was crazy. It was like He was with them, which He promised He would be.

Some people flocked to them. They were healing, sharing, and telling people how to connect with their heavenly Father in a way that bypassed all the corrupt ritualistic forms and politically motivated religious leaders. A freedom that was not subject to economic or social status. There were no barriers beyond belief.

Others were wary. All this fuss over a Messiah who was killed by the enemy He was supposed to overthrow. It didn't make sense. Plus, movements like this had started before and fizzled out. They took a wait-and-see approach.

Still others were downright hostile. This whole thing sounded like a total overhaul of a system that was working for them. The Romans were content to leave them alone as long as they paid their taxes and kept quiet. Too much rocking the boat might lead to trouble. But these Christians would not shut up.

Everywhere they went, it was "Jesus this" and "Jesus that" and "You had Him killed, but He came back to life, which proves you were wrong about Him." They wanted to tear the whole system down and replace it with . . . what? A group of people who gather together to sing, pray, worship, and share? That sounded like crazy talk. Next thing you know they'll let women and Gentiles in their club.

They tried to shut it down, but that only made it grow faster. It started spreading from Jerusalem to the rest of Judea to Samaria and eventually to the ends of the earth.

And now here we are. No matter our age, our status, our nationality, our location, our bank account, our wardrobe, our haircut, our eye color . . . we are bound together as members of one church. Because of this crazy, unprecedented plan that, practically speaking, had no chance of working.

Power Trip

Jesus' whole deal was to restore humanity's relationship with God. He told people that God cared about them individually. He came to tell people they could know God personally, as their heavenly Father—which meant they were His children. His message was not just meant for the few fortunate people who lived in Israel back then; His message was meant for the whole world.

And yet He chose to come to earth at a time when there was no Internet, no cable TV news outlets, no social media. There were a few decent roads but no automobiles, let alone any airplanes. He only stayed for a little while, and then He left His mission in the hands of eleven guys who didn't know what they were doing.

If God really wanted to communicate His message to the entire world, it seems like God could have come up with a better plan than that. But He comes to earth as a single Guy, tells people about His plan for a few years, mentors twelve guys (one of whom commits suicide), and He leaves—telling them to keep up the good work. It was the ultimate power trip that would change the course of history, offering salvation freely and extravagantly.

This does not make sense. Jesus did not attend a marketing class or maximize His platform. Jesus seems to prefer deep to wide. He prefers personal relationships to mass communication. And then He leaves just as the whole thing really gets going, leaving things in the hands of eleven highly underqualified men. This sounds like the worst strategy ever. It's certainly not how I would have done it. Frankly, with this plan, it's surprising that the whole Christian movement survived the first century.

But this is God's plan to rescue the world: the church. That's it. Not a corporation or a university, not a nation or an economic strategy. Simply, His church. The followers He left behind would tell others. Then they would tell others, generation after generation.

I've got to give it to those early followers; they bet the farm on Jesus. They went all in. Many of them ended up dying for it. They endured persecution, humiliation, and even martyrdom for this ridiculous plan. Yes, it got sideways. Yes, a thing that started as a movement became an institution. Yes, terrible things were done. The church became political. The church got interested in manipulation and power. The church came to think it existed for insiders. The church started to reject and repel the kinds of people who gravitated to Jesus.

But Jesus had made a promise. He had told His friends He would build a church the gates of hell would not be able to stop. And since its inception there has always been a remnant of people who get it—who understand that movements are meant to move—who knew that the church was not originally for "church people" because there were no church people.

There have been missionaries, Bible translators, evangelists, smugglers, preachers, teachers, servants, and caretakers who knew this message must spread. There have always been people who knew this wasn't about a location, control, or hierarchy. There have always been people who knew that the church is God's plan to rescue the world, so they've met in caves, living rooms, or hotel ballrooms—wherever two or more can gather. They serve the poor, hold babies, and baptize people. They move, they go, and they grow—as does the church accordingly.

And the really crazy thing is that it's actually working.

That Time God Became a Fetus

AS YOU CAN tell from the previous chapters of this book, God does a lot of crazy things. At least they seem crazy from our perspective, and it takes some deeper thinking to see how sane some of the crazy-seeming things might actually be.

He tried to kill Moses. He sent a giant fish to swallow Jonah. He made a donkey talk. He told Abraham to kill his only son. He had Hosea marry a prostitute. But without a doubt the single most unsettling, irrational, illogical thing He ever did was the time He came to earth as a baby. If He had come as a full-grown man, I might understand that a little better. If He had come as an angel, a ghost, an apparition, or a disembodied voice, it might make more sense—at least it might have fit our expectations a little better.

But a completely helpless baby? He couldn't feed Himself, talk, walk, or control His own bladder. And have you ever witnessed a birth? It's not for the fainthearted. Sure it's wonderful, amazing, beautiful, and life affirming—tell yourself that if you want. I've been to three of them, and I got queasy.

But that's how God chose to enter the world. He could have chosen any means—something miraculous and exceptional, regal and majestic. But He chose the ordinary way.

Worse than that, He chose to enter as a peasant, in a barn, in a backwater town, with nothing but a carpenter's rough and calloused hands to usher Him into the world. This couple, miles away from home, unable to find a decent place to sleep, spends the night in a stable, or perhaps it was a barn or cave—we know it was where animals were kept. More than likely there were insects and certainly manure. The teenage mother goes into labor and delivers a Baby that has already caused her so much pain . . . and will cause even more in His attempt to bring true peace, true healing, true joy.

There were no kingly satin bed sheets, no velvet onesies for this Prince. No hand-carved ivory crèche or golden rattle for His hand. Just strips of cloth to keep Him warm as Mary's husband makes room for the Baby in an empty feeding trough. That's where they put our God—the Author of life, the King of kings, the Prince of peace—lying there among the spittle and leftover animal feed. There may have been more animals than people present.

In fact, no other people showed up except a few dirty shepherds and some strange guys from the East who arrived several months, if not years, later. It doesn't make much sense—the God of the universe humbling Himself in such a way, emptying Himself of so much for so little in return. This tiny bundle of joy lying there in the middle of a big mess—that's our God.

Jesus was born while the family was on the road, and there was something of a commotion immediately after the blessed event. Angels sang, and the aforementioned shepherds came out of the fields with a crazy story of their own. Strange travelers from the East showed up to worship the new King of the Jews (which sent the current king of the Jews into a tizzy). Babies were killed, and the family fled to Egypt for a while. When they returned, they settled in a town called Nazareth, in the hill country of Galilee. Jesus was in some respects what we might call a hillbilly.

He would have gone to school, learning to read and write. That means God learned from humans. If that doesn't blow your mind, you didn't read it right. God learned from humans how to read and write. He studied. He learned a trade from His father and worked in the family business. He grew taller. His life had a crazy beginning, but maybe the craziest thing is how normal most of His childhood would have been, based on what we know. Oh, except for the fact that He was actually God in a body!

He was born in a mess, wrapped in rags, laid in a manger. Then He died in a mess, stripped of His rags, hung on a cross. And in between those two events, He mostly hung out with messy people. He had developed a reputation for doing the wrong things with the right people and the right things with the wrong people. He hung out with prostitutes and tax collectors, the seediest of the seedy. He seemed equally at home with religious leaders and outcasts. His best friends weren't very educated and probably lacked some of the social graces we often prefer. He talks respectfully with women. He plays with children. He touches lepers. He cries in public. Then, as if none of this is crazy enough, He lets the people He created torture and murder Him. God in a body dies, and it's not a very dignified death. If you thought the circumstances of His birth were scandalous, the circumstances of His death go to a whole new level of scandal. But that is our God—make no mistake. This is how He wanted it, how He planned it. He risked everything in order to rescue the people who have never been able to keep their promises to Him. He proved definitively that this really is His crazy story.

Man, Myths, and Truth

I went through a phase when I was fascinated by Greek mythology. I remember reading about how the gods would sometimes come to earth in disguise and interact with humans. Then they'd return to Mount Olympus. It was fun to imagine. But I never thought it was real. In fact, I thought the Greek people must have been really dumb to believe this stuff. No one would ever believe that all-powerful gods—who created and maintained everything—would come down from their palatial estates disguised as humans and walk among us. It never occurred to me that the New Testament begins with this premise.

God goes in an instant from the most beautiful and comfortable place imaginable to the womb of a teenage girl. Nine months later He arrives while she's on a road trip to her fiancée's hometown. The only place to put Him is in a feeding trough. He lives for a few decades, walking around in His earth suit.

This has some unsettling implications. Earth suits leak. They're ticklish and stinky. God put one of these things on. He sweated, cried, laughed, and all the other things our bodies do. He was exposed to germs, experienced physical pain, was injured, and died. What kind of God does that? What kind of God humbles Himself to the point of living with the restrictions of a human body?

Ancient Greeks loved power. They talked about power and thought about power. They would dream about what they would do if they had absolute power. For them power was the highest attribute of all. Power was even greater than morality. They figured that if a god were to submit to a code of morality, then that god must be inferior to that code or whoever might enforce that code or whoever codified the code in the first place. A god wasn't supposed to be inferior to anything, so the gods in Greek mythology periodically broke their promises—just to prove that they could do whatever they wanted and no one could say "boo" about it. They were capricious; they loved to flex their muscles and show people who was in charge. They threw lightning bolts down on a poor mortal just because they could. They made laws and broke them, and if you questioned them, they'd send a pox on your house!

But the God we meet in the pages of Scripture isn't like that. This YHWH comes to Abraham with a promise. By making that promise, God was intentionally limiting His power. By entering into a covenant, God eliminated a lot of possible actions on His part. He could not *not* bless Abraham's descendants; He had committed Himself to a particular course of action. The God of the Bible seems to think the willing restraint of power—we might call that *humility*—is a greater attribute than the possession of absolute power. He knows it's an immature person who feels the need to constantly flex his muscles to impress people. Mature people can practice self-control.

There's no better example of this than the life of Jesus, particularly when He is tempted in the wilderness. Satan tries to get Him to do three things that would have been simple enough for Jesus to do, and Jesus refuses. Even after Satan offers to transfer ownership of all the kingdoms of earth to Him, Jesus still refuses.

You see, Jesus understood that people don't need a God who can flex His muscles for His own benefit; people need a God who will keep His promises and use His power for their benefit.

Yes, ancient Greeks loved power. But thankfully, our God loves people.

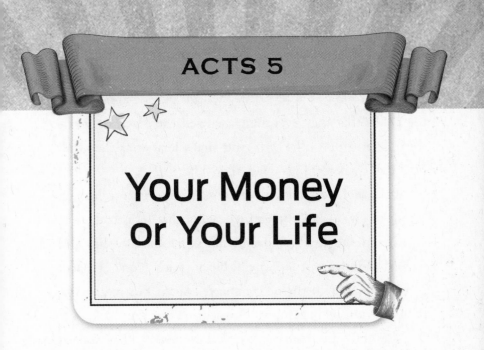

ACTS 5

Your Money or Your Life

THIS WHOLE CHURCH thing started with a traveling Rabbi named Jesus who was teaching, preaching, healing, and performing various miracles. He drew some really big crowds; the more people listened to Him, however, the more the religious leaders grew to distrust Him. They thought Jesus was perverting their religion by watering it down. And you know how weird people can get about their religion.

Time and again Jesus assured them that He wasn't trying to twist their religion; rather, He was straightening it out. What was really frustrating was how He used the old writings of Moses, King David, and the prophets to back up what He was saying. Many of the religious leaders had no response, much less a valid one; for them it was maddening.

So they tried to trap Him with gotcha questions and mind games, but He was always a step ahead. He got so far under their skin that they eventually realized there was only one thing left to do: kill Him. And that's just what they did. And that's when things got really weird.

At first His disciples all scattered and went into hiding. Then rumors began circulating, saying that Jesus had come back from the dead. A dead man came back to life and walked the streets of Jerusalem. He ate with people. He had conversations with them. He showed them His scars. And then He vanished again.

Now His disciples weren't slinking away. They started preaching, teaching, healing, and doing all the same sorts of things Jesus had done. The religious leaders didn't like it any more the second time around, so they resolved to round up Jesus' friends and have them suffer the same fate as their Leader. The problem was, the more they hunted down, the more there were. These Christians weren't just adding; they were multiplying.

Ananias and Sapphira were part of that group. Like so many others, they were captivated by the message of Jesus, the message of a Man who gave everything for others and said there was nothing better than to sacrifice yourself for your friends. They were probably blown away to discover that the people following Jesus, this movement called "church" people, were actually doing what Jesus said. They were giving away their lives and possessions for one another.

One day Ananias and Sapphira saw a man named Joseph (everyone called him "the son of encouragement") give a bunch of money to the church. He said he wanted to help make sure no needy person would go without assistance so he sold a parcel of land and gave all the proceeds. Perhaps they were swept up in the emotion of the moment; maybe they liked the feeling that comes when you decide to give something big away. Maybe they legitimately wanted to help people. We don't know. For some reason, however, they decided to do the same thing they'd seen Joseph do.

They went out and sold a piece of land, and they brought *some* of the money to the church. If that was all they did, we probably wouldn't be talking about them now. But we know what happened—they went one step too far and told people that what they'd brought was the *entire* amount.

Cue the dramatic music.

Peter, the leader of the church, smells a rat. There was no need to lie. He confronts Ananias, reminding him that the property was his and that he could have done whatever he wanted with both the property and the proceeds. And then Ananias falls down dead. Boom!

Sapphira enters, has the same conversation with Peter, and now the church is planning its first double funeral.

The story ends with what surely must be one of the great understatements in all of Scripture, "Then great fear came on the whole church and on all who heard these things" (Acts 5:11).

There Goes the Neighborhood

Is anyone else as uncomfortable with this crazy story as I am? God killed this couple, and there's just no way of pretending He didn't. Ananias and Sapphira probably seemed like a nice couple—the kind of people you want to live next door to. You might invite them over for a cookout. You'd probably ask them to check your mail for you while you're on vacation.

I bet if this had happened in modern times, their neighbors would have noticed when the newspapers started piling up in the driveway. And the porch light had been left on for several days. I'm trying to imagine what must have gone through the minds of their neighbors when they started asking around about where Ananias and Sapphira had gone, only to hear that they were dead. Surely their friends and coworkers wanted to know how they died.

God killed them. Wait . . . what?

Granted, the process of "joining a church" was still fairly new, but did anyone ever think that doing so might be lethal?

Most of us are comfortable with the idea that life is God's to give and take as He sees fit; He determines where and how long we live. That's not what's bothersome to me. What's bothersome to me is . . . well, maybe I should back up a little first.

Jesus came into the world proclaiming the kingdom of God, and part of this kingdom is a commitment to radical generosity. Look hard enough, and you'll see that at or near the core of everything Jesus taught His followers. He started His ministry by saying He had come "to preach good news to the poor . . . to proclaim freedom to the captives and recovery of sight to the blind, to set free the oppressed" (Luke 4:18).

That never meant Jesus would minister exclusively to the downtrodden, but it did mean He chose to invest in the lives of people who could provide Him nothing in return. Now, *that's* generosity. And with everything else He did, it's easy for us to overlook the radical nature of His generosity. In one of His stories (found in Matt. 20), a man hires some day laborers. The man picks up a crew in the morning, and they agree on payment. Then he picks up another crew later in the day and still another crew near sunset. When the time for payment comes, however, he pays everyone the same amount. Now if you and I were part of the morning crew that had worked all day, this would hardly seem fair!

But that whole story is about how generous Jesus is. And when Jesus says, "Follow me," He expects us to follow Him into that kind of generosity. He really did say, "No one has greater love than this, that someone would lay down his life for his friends" (John 15:13). That means there is no end to generosity; you and I cannot give too much.

Maybe what's most amazing about this story is that the early church believed they were actually supposed to do stuff like this. We're told, "Now the large group of those who believed were of one heart and mind, and no one said that any of his possessions was his own, but instead they held everything in common" (Acts 4:32).

No one had to enforce this. They heard what Jesus said, and they did it. Following Jesus into generosity was a no-brainer for them. They figured Jesus was generous, so we will be generous, too. How could you look at what Jesus did, hear what He said, and do the opposite?

I once heard a friend define *greed* as "the assumption that it's all for my consumption." He meant that every gift we've received, whether we think we worked for it or not, filters its way through our minds as if it were created for our personal consumption. What's mine is mine, and you can't have it. Maybe this is why surveys show that the average Christian gives less than 2.5 percent of their income (that includes what they give to their local church and to charities

. . . combined). I'll even hear some people say things like, "I tithe 5 percent."

OK, I don't want to get into a big conversation about tithing and whether or not it's "required," but I do want to point this out: *a tithe is a tenth*. That's what the word means. You cannot "tithe 5 percent" without changing the meaning of the word. Have we lost the spirit of generosity to such an extent that we no longer even know the vocabulary?

Generosity is a Jesus thing, but that's not the reason God killed Ananias and Sapphira. He killed them because they lied. As Peter is dressing down Ananias, he says, "You have not lied to men but to God!" (Acts 5:4).

Now I know lots of people lie in church. I bet your pastor has done it. I know I've done it. There would be no youth pastors in America if everyone who lied in church were suddenly struck dead! So there's got to be more going on here, right?

Again Peter's words hold a clue. He begins his message by asking, "Ananias, why has Satan filled your heart to lie to the Holy Spirit and keep back part of the proceeds from the field?" (Acts 5:3). He says Satan hasn't just tempted them to lie; Satan has filled their hearts. The heart of a believer is reserved for the Holy Spirit.

This tragic story has nothing to do with God's being cavalier or capricious; Satan and the Holy Spirit are wholly incompatible. A house divided against itself cannot stand,

and neither could Ananias and Sapphira. This couple had not embraced the way of life envisioned and practiced by Jesus. They weren't concerned with the way of Jesus—a way marked by generosity, grace, love, and, yes, suffering. They just wanted to pretend they were. And God hates pretending.

In fact, God hates hypocrisy. God prefers honest disagreement to dishonest posing. Had they simply been honest about where they were in their journey and what they were willing to give, they'd have stayed alive. They weren't required to give the entire profit from the sale of the land, but they wanted to receive credit for having done so.

My guess is that most of us are pretending at something right now. "Fake it 'til you make it" is sage advice sometimes but not in church. God can't be faked out. He sees straight through all the pious posturing into these hearts of ours.

God can take whatever you can part with right now and walk you into a deeper experience with Him. If you're not "there" yet, don't pretend you are. If you do, you might want to make sure your will is up-to-date.

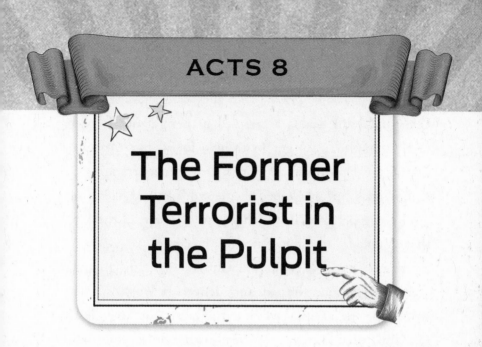

ACTS 8

The Former Terrorist in the Pulpit

OSAMA BIN LADEN is dead. I saw the movie. They got him. There's a part of me that is glad the world is rid of someone who was so evil and destructive. Another part of me finds it hard to rejoice in the death of anyone—even someone so treacherous and diabolical as OBL. The reason for my mixed feelings lies within our next crazy story.

Shortly after Jesus left the earth, His followers started gaining traction with a simple message: Jesus is who He claimed to be, and the fact that He came back to life after His crucifixion proves it. That was their message. Short. Simple.

It had implications, however, and they did spend some time trying to figure it out, but mostly they stuck to the facts. Jesus died. God vindicated Him by bringing Him back to life. People saw it. And then a miracle happened. Peter and John healed a crippled man right on the steps of the temple. They got in trouble for it, but they used that as an opportunity to preach that same sermon again. Thousands of people joined them, and it looked like things were going pretty well, which is always a sign in the Bible that trouble is lurking just around the corner.

One of the leaders of the church was a man named Stephen. He gets arrested and delivers a long and fiery speech that ends with the familiar refrain: "You killed Jesus, but God raised Him up. Now deal with those implications." They dealt with it by throwing rocks at Stephen until he was dead.

The Bible tells us there was a young man there named Saul. Saul was a crazy dude. He didn't just oppose Christianity; he wanted to hunt down Christians and kill them. All of them. But one day Saul had a crazy thing happen to him: Jesus appeared to him, knocked him off his high horse, and struck him blind. Saul had no idea what was going on; he only knew that he once could see but now was blind. Jesus tells him to go visit a man in the next city, a city where Saul was headed to catch more Christians. The man prays for Saul, and he is able to see again. This is when Saul starts to rethink his role in the whole Jesus movement. Maybe murdering Christians isn't how he wants to spend the rest of his days. Before long Saul has changed his name to Paul and starts preaching about Jesus. Not only that, Paul becomes a very passionate Christian. He starts dozens of churches, spreading the news about Jesus around the world—including non-Jews in this message of hope. He even writes most of the New Testament.

This guy goes from being the worst man alive to being the most sought-after teacher in Christendom. He spends the rest of his days telling other Christians what it means to be a Christian. Everywhere he travels, he tells everyone he meets about Jesus. He even has this crazy idea that if he could get to the emperor—that's right, the emperor of Rome—he might be able to persuade him that Jesus really is who He claimed to be. How cool would it be to convert the most powerful man in the world to Christianity? That's who Paul became: champion of the gospel, evangelist to the Gentiles. This man who used to focus on destroying all Christians.

About-Face

What happened with Paul was crazy, and—yet again—one of the things that makes it crazy is that we act as if this is the most normal thing in the world. Ho-hum. This Paul guy goes from having Christians arrested, beaten, tortured, and killed to being one of them. And they accept him. No big deal.

Um, yes it is a big deal. Sane and rational people must have thought, *Paul? That guy killed my brother. Are we sure we want him to speak at the men's breakfast next week? Who thought this was a good idea?* Normal people would not do something like that. But Christians, especially the ones we read about in the book of Acts, are not normal. They do not believe normal beliefs, and they do not behave in normal ways. Christians are called to be abnormal—to buck the trends of our surrounding culture when they come into conflict with the values of God's kingdom.

And that brings me back to Osama bin Laden and my mixed feelings about his death.

Can you imagine how crazy it would have been if Seal Team 6 had captured him instead of killing him? Suppose they captured him and brought him to the United States, and when he got here he said, "You know what? I was totally wrong about America and Americans. I think I'd like to apply for citizenship."

Now imagine our government saying, "Sure you can become a citizen. All is forgiven. Why not run for public office while you're at it?" He says, "I think I will." And he becomes the mayor of Detroit, bringing that once proud bastion of American industry back to life. He becomes so successful at turning things around that other civic leaders seek his advice on the best way to run a city. Then governors start to call. Then the president asks him to serve on a special council. He goes down in history as one of our greatest leaders and advocates for truth, justice, and the American way. Cue the music. Unfurl the flags. Light the fireworks.

On second thought, no. Hold everything. That would never happen. That's too crazy. There is no way the American people would forgive him. There is no way he would be allowed to visit America. There would have been riots in the streets. There was even less of a chance he'd be granted citizenship. And even less of a chance he'd be allowed to run for public office. And even less of a chance that he'd win. The whole idea is ridiculous.

And yet the earliest Christians allowed their worst enemy to reverse himself, to change his mind, to do a 180 and take a mulligan on the whole "hunt them down and kill them" thing. They let him travel. They let him teach. They let him become a leader in the church. How in the world did that happen?

Because those Christians assumed a bad person could legitimately change. They knew that a bad person wasn't destined to stay a bad person. They knew that liars, adulterers and, yes, even murderers could experience real transformation because of the power of God. They refused to believe Saul's past would define his future. They did not agree that the best predictor of future performance is past behavior. They believed that God could change people, that God wanted to change people, that God's greatest desire was to take totally depraved people and remake them into the saints they were designed to be.

So they gave this Paul guy a shot. Maybe they were skeptical; maybe they assigned Barnabas to him as a chaperone because they weren't completely convinced. But they were open to the possibility that the grace of God might actually be able to accomplish that kind of change in a person's life.

Have we lost that today? Have we stopped believing in a God who can and does change the very nature of a person? Do we still believe God could have changed the heart of someone like Osama bin Laden? Do we even bother to pray for that?

Can God still save a person? Can God still pierce a person's heart? Is that kind of transformation still possible? And finally, would we believe it if it happened?

Epilogue

THERE IS A real danger in reading a book like this—a book filled with stories that seem unbelievable but, being contained in the Bible, must, therefore, be accepted as true by every good, conservative, evangelical believer. Reading a book like this is dangerous for two reasons, one positive and one negative.

Negatively speaking, the danger of a book like this is that you might read it, learn a bit, and set it aside. You might think, *Wow! God sure did a lot of crazy things back in Bible times! I'm glad He grew out of that phase.*

You might take all these great stories about talking donkeys and UFOs and angry bears and put them in the file labeled *church* and only open that file a couple of times a week. You might memorize a few pieces of trivia and trot those out to impress your small group sometime. You might think, from time to time, about what it must have been like to live during a time when God did crazy things, and then you might wake up from your daydreams and return to your regularly scheduled programming.

Please don't do that. It's dangerous.

I grew up in a faith heritage that was part of what's known as the American Restoration Movement. We were earnest in our desire to restore New Testament Christianity, but we had our limits. We wanted to restore the forms of the early church; we were less concerned about restoring the beliefs of the early church.

Specifically, we were quick to affirm that God did all of these crazy things back then, before the Bible was written. Now that we have the Bible, God doesn't have to do crazy things anymore. We never said it that way, but it's what we all believed. God had stopped doing all that, and for that we were ever so grateful.

We would not have believed Saul's conversion if it had happened today. We believed it because it happened back then when God "did that kind of thing." We would not have believed Ezekiel's vision. We would have explained away the bears and the great fish and the demonic pigs. We would have told Abraham he was wrong. We would have suggested that Moses had heatstroke. We would have sought out a medical explanation for King Nebuchadnezzar. We did not believe God did crazy things anymore.

Because we did not believe these things occurred, we never bothered to pray for God to change the hearts of politicians or celebrities or to intervene much in our affairs beyond "being with" sick people and giving us safe travels to whatever mission trip we were taking that summer. We complained about Hollywood without ever considering that God might want us to partner with Him in redeeming it. No, we believed God was done with all the over-the-top, unbelievable stories we read about every Sunday. "I once was blind but now I see" was something we sang but only meant metaphorically now. We expected blind people to stay blind and lost people to stay lost. Dead people stayed dead, and there was nothing to be done about it.

But it's dangerous to draw a line through human history and say, "God used to be like that; now He's like this." God hasn't changed. He's still willing to go to ridiculous lengths to get our attention, and there remains no one—absolutely no one—who is too far away for His grace to reach.

We dare not believe God used to be able to use crazy things like animals and dreams and performance artists to get our attention and communicate His message. We dare not limit the God of the universe. He still does as He pleases, and He has never taken very kindly to those who say, "God can't anymore."

Leaving all these crazy stories in the past would be dangerous, but that wouldn't be the greatest danger of reading a book like this.

Now, before I tell you what I think the greatest danger would be, I want to remind you of something: just because a thing is dangerous does not make it bad. There are lots of things that are good, but they are dangerous. Fire is like that. Driving a car is like that. Ministry is like that—it's good, but it's dangerous.

So, having said that, here is what I want to leave you with: the greatest danger of reading a book like this is that you might begin to believe God may have another crazy story or two up His anthropomorphic sleeve. You might even begin praying and looking for some crazy story to happen, something involving our current president or another world leader coming to faith and legislating like one who has been captured by the matchless grace of Jesus. Or a celebrity using his or her influence to advance God's agenda in our world.

You might begin living out a crazy story of your own. You might sell some of your stuff and give the money to the poor. You might go to a developing nation on a mission trip and decide never to come back. You might sponsor children and volunteer as a mentor and begin to extend the borders of God's kingdom in your generation. You might worship God with such great abandonment that the people in the pews around you move to another section of the sanctuary. You might inspire others to live in freedom and pray for freedom and work toward freedom. You might get a group of your friends to move with you into the inner city and begin cleaning things up.

You might even begin to live as if this crazy story of a God who creates out of abundance, and whose default setting is to bless, and who loves with such abandon that He relentlessly pursues us until we surrender to His greatness and His goodness as if it just might be true. If you did surrender to a God like that, you might find yourself living like He lives, seeing people as He sees them and treating them as He has treated you.

That would be dangerous indeed.

Here's my hunch: I think a lot of people who are reading this book could look back at their own lives and say, "This has been one crazy story!" There's been at least one episode in your life that doesn't make sense unless the lid is off the universe and there's a God who periodically reaches in to adjust our circumstances.

I know this is true for me. It's true for just about everyone I meet. So here's what I'd like you to do: go to my website (www.johnalanturner.com) and share your crazy story with the world. I think going public with the crazy things God has done in our own lives may actually inspire more crazy stories.

And, if there's anything I think the world needs more of, it's the good kind of crazy/dangerous stories that happen when God's people wake up every morning and say, "God, You show me where to go and what to do today, and I'll be brave enough to do it because I do not want to miss the adventure You have in store for me!"

These are the kinds of stories the apostles told that launched a church that has traveled to the ends of the earth; and these are the kinds of stories those of us who have read the Bible twenty times still need to hear. If there's anything we can be honest about having read what we've just read, it's this: the cast of characters in God's story look a lot more like the cast of *Mad Men* or *Sons of Anarchy* than we care to admit. God would rather use broken and jacked up people than superficial types dressed to impress in their Sunday best.

Own your crazy story. Go live it for the glory of the One who made you and redeemed you and has promised to see to it that everything works out for your good.